150 PERFECT DESSERT RECIPES

150 PERFECT
DESSERT RECIPES

Sara Lewis

For Sian, a few ideas to help broaden your repertoire!

An Hachette UK Company
www.hachette.co.uk

First published in Great Britain in 2009 by
Hamlyn, a division of Octopus Publishing Group Ltd,
Endeavour House, 189 Shaftesbury Avenue, WC2H 8JY
www.octopusbooks.co.uk

This exclusive edition published in 2011

ISBN: 978-0-600-62426-4

A CIP catalogue record for this book is available
from the British Library.

Printed and bound in China

1 2 3 4 5 6 7 8 9 10

Both metric and imperial measurements are given in all
recipes. Use one set of measurements, not a mixture of both.

Standard level spoon measurements are used in all recipes
1 tablespoon = one 15 ml spoon
1 teaspoon = one 5 ml spoon

Ovens should be preheated to the specified temperature – if
using a fan-assisted oven, follow the manufacturer's
instructions for adjusting the time and the temperature.

Milk should be full fat unless otherwise stated.

Eggs should be medium unless otherwise stated. The
Department of Health advises that eggs should not be
consumed raw. This book contains some dishes made with
raw or lightly cooked eggs. It is prudent for vulnerable
people such as pregnant and nursing mothers, invalids, the
elderly, babies and young children to avoid uncooked or
lightly cooked dishes made with eggs. Once prepared, these
dishes should be kept refrigerated and used promptly.

This book also includes dishes made with nuts and nut
derivatives. It is advisable for those with known allergic
reactions to nuts and nut derivatives and those who may be
potentially vulnerable to these allergies, such as pregnant
and nursing mothers, invalids, the elderly, babies and
children to avoid dishes made with nuts and nut oils. It is
also prudent to check the labels of pre–prepared ingredients
for the possible inclusion of nut derivatives.

contents

introduction

Not many people can resist a dessert. A good one will cheer you up after a bad day at work, banish the blues and make a grand finale to a special meal or a welcome gift when visiting friends for supper.

tips & tricks
making meringues
The bowl and whisk must be dry and grease-free. If you drop any yolk into the whites when separating the eggs, scoop it out with a piece of shell, as even the tiniest amount of yolk will prevent the whites from whisking.
1 Whisk the whites until very thick so they will stand in moist-looking peaks. If you're not sure if they're ready, turn the bowl upside down – if the egg whites stay put, they're ready; if they begin to slide out, whisk a little more.

2 Gradually whisk in the sugar a teaspoonful at a time. When all the sugar has been added, whisk for a couple more minutes until the meringue is very thick and glossy.
3 Shape the meringues by spooning or spreading on to a baking sheet lined with nonstick baking paper, and bake according to the recipe until the meringues are crisp and may be easily lifted off the paper. If they stick to the paper, return them to the oven for 10–20 minutes and test again.

working with chocolate
To melt chocolate, break it into pieces and heat for 5 minutes or so in a bowl set over a saucepan of very gently simmering water, making sure that the water doesn't touch the base of the bowl. Stir just before using.

Decorative chocolate curls are easy to make using a swivel-bladed vegetable peeler. Place a bar of chocolate on a chopping board with the smooth underside uppermost. Run the vegetable peeler blade along the top of the chocolate with the handle almost touching the edge of the bar. If the curls are too small, warm the chocolate in 10-second bursts in the microwave on full power (or in a warm oven) and try again. As the chocolate softens, the curls will increase in size.

baking blind
This rather strange term really just means to bake the tart case empty.

1 Stand the tart tin on a baking sheet, then prick the pastry base with a fork.

2 Line with crumpled nonstick or greaseproof paper. Half-fill the tin with dried macaroni or baking beans to hold the pastry in shape.

3 Bake at 190°C (375°F), Gas Mark 5, for 10–15 minutes until just set, then lift out the paper and filling. Cook the empty tart for 5 more minutes until golden around the top edges and the base is dry and crisp, or for 10 minutes if the filling will not be cooked.

This recipe makes enough to fill a 25 cm (10 inch) flan tin or 450 g (14½ oz) pastry.

250 g (8 oz) **plain flour**, plus extra for dusting
25 g (1 oz) **icing sugar**
125 g (4 oz) mix of **unsalted butter** and **white vegetable fat**, or all butter, diced
8–9 teaspoons cold **water**

Place the flour and sugar in a bowl, add the sugar and diced fats and rub in with the fingertips until the mixture resembles fine breadcrumbs. (For speed, use an electric mixer or food processor.) Add 8 teaspoons cold water and mix with a round-bladed knife until the crumbs begin to clump together, then squeeze with the fingertips, adding an extra teaspoon of water if needed to bring the mixture together to a ball. Knead lightly on a lightly floured surface then chill, wrapped in

clingfilm, for 15 minutes, or if preferred roll out, line a tart tin and chill. If chilled, the pastry relaxes and shrinks less when baked.

flaky pastry

This recipe makes enough to top a 1.2 litre (2 pint) pie dish or 500 g (1 lb) pastry.

250 g (8 oz) **plain flour**, plus extra for dusting
pinch **salt**
75 g (3 oz) **lard** or **white pastry fat**
75 g (3 oz) **unsalted butter**
2 teaspoons **lemon juice**
5–6 tablespoons cold **water**

Place the flour and salt in a mixing bowl, add one quarter of the white fat and one quarter of the butter and rub in with the fingertips until the mixture resembles fine breadcrumbs. Add the lemon juice then enough cold water, mixing with a round-bladed knife, to form a soft but not sticky dough. Knead lightly, then roll out on a floured surface to form a rough rectangle, about 46 x 15 cm (18 x 6 inches). Dot half the remaining white fat and butter over the bottom two-thirds of the pastry. Fold over the top one-third of the dough and then fold up the bottom third to enclose the fat. Press the edges together well, then give the dough a quarter turn. Roll out the pastry again, dot with fats and fold, as before. Give a quarter turn, then roll and fold twice more. Wrap in clingfilm and chill for 30 minutes.

lemon puddle pudding

Serves **4**
Preparation time **20 minutes**
Cooking time **25 minutes**

75 g (3 oz) **unsalted butter**,
   at room temperature
150 g (5 oz) **caster sugar**
grated rind of 2 **lemons**, plus
   juice from 1 lemon
3 **eggs**, separated
50 g (2 oz) **self-raising flour**
300 ml (½ pint) **milk**
icing sugar, for dusting
   (optional)

Grease a 1.2 litre (2 pint) pie dish lightly, then stand the dish in a roasting tin. Put the rest of the butter in a mixing bowl with the sugar and lemon rind. Whisk the egg whites in a separate bowl until they are softly peaking. Using the still dirty whisk, beat the butter, sugar and lemon rind until light and fluffy, then mix in the flour and egg yolks.

Mix in the milk and lemon juice gradually until only just mixed. The mixture may appear to separate slightly but this will disappear during baking.

Fold in the egg whites, then gently pour the mix into the greased dish. Pour hot water from the tap into the roasting tin to come halfway up the sides of the dish.

Cook in a preheated oven, 190°C (375°F), Gas Mark 5, for about 25 minutes until slightly risen, golden brown and the top has begun to crack. Insert a knife into the centre – the top two-thirds should be soufflé-like and the bottom third a saucy, custard-like layer. If it's very soft in the centre, cook for an extra 5 minutes.

Dust the top with a little sifted icing sugar, if liked, then serve immediately spooned into shallow bowls. Don't leave the dessert to stand or the topping will absorb the sauce.

For Grand Marnier pudding, use the grated rind of 1 large orange instead of the lemon rind and replace the lemon juice with 3 tablespoons Grand Marnier. Cook as above.

roasted pears with oriental spices

Serves **4**
Preparation time **20 minutes**
Cooking time **25 minutes**

4 **pears**
8 tablespoons **dry** or **sweet sherry**
8 tablespoons **water**
6–8 pieces **star anise**
1 **cinnamon stick**, broken into pieces
8 **cloves**
8 **cardamom pods**, crushed
50 g (2 oz) **unsalted butter**
4 tablespoons **light muscovado sugar**
1 **orange**

Leave the peel on the pears and cut them in half, down through the stems to the base. Scoop out the core, then put in a roasting tin with the cut sides up. Spoon the sherry into the core cavity of each pear and the water into the base of the tin. Sprinkle the spices over the pears, including the cardamom pods and their black seeds. Dot with the butter, then sprinkle with the sugar.

Remove the rind from the orange and sprinkle into the tin. Cut the orange into wedges and squeeze the juice over the pears. Add the wedges to the base of the roasting tin.

Cook in a preheated oven, 180°C (350°F), Gas Mark 4, for 25 minutes until tender and just beginning to brown, spooning the pan juices over the pears halfway through cooking and again at the end.

Spoon into shallow dishes, drizzle with the pan juices and serve with crème fraîche or Greek yogurt.

For roast apples with peppercorns, core and halve 4 dessert apples, then place, cut side up, in a roasting tin. Spoon 200 ml (7 fl oz) cider over the apples and into the roasting tin. Sprinkle with 1 teaspoon coarsely crushed multicoloured peppercorns and 1 broken cinnamon stick. Dot with butter and sprinkle with sugar as above. Remove the rind from 1 lemon and reserve for decoration, then cut the lemon into wedges, squeeze the juice over the apples and add the wedges to the base of the tin. Bake as above.

sticky toffee puddings

Makes **8**
Preparation time **20 minutes**
Cooking time **45–50 minutes**

125 g (4 oz) pitted chopped
   dried dates
150 ml (¼ pint) **water**
125 g (4 oz) **unsalted butter**,
   softened
125 g (4 oz) **caster sugar**
1 teaspoon **vanilla essence**
3 **eggs**
175 g (6 oz) **self-raising flour**
1 teaspoon **baking powder**

Toffee sauce
300 ml (½ pint) **double cream**
125 g (4 oz) **light brown**
   sugar
50 g (2 oz) **unsalted butter**

Put the dates in a small pan with the measured water and simmer gently for 5 minutes until the dates are soft and pulpy. Blend to a purée, then allow to cool.

Make the sauce. Heat half the cream in a small, heavy-bottomed pan with the sugar and butter until the sugar dissolves. Bring to the boil, then let the sauce bubble for about 5 minutes until a rich, dark caramel. Stir in the remaining cream and set aside.

Grease 8 metal 200 ml (7 fl oz) pudding moulds and line the bottoms with nonstick baking paper. Beat the butter, sugar, vanilla essence, eggs, flour and baking powder in a bowl for 1–2 minutes until pale and creamy. Stir the date purée into the pudding mixture.

Divide the mixture among the moulds. Level the tops and place in a roasting tin. Pour boiling water to a depth of 1.5 cm (¾ inch) in the tin and cover with foil. Bake in a preheated oven, 180°C (350°F), Gas Mark 4, for 35–40 minutes or until risen and firm to the touch.

Leave the puddings in the moulds while you reheat the sauce, then loosen the edges of the moulds and invert the puddings on to serving plates. Cover with sauce and serve with additional cream or ice cream.

For gingered figgy puddings, cook 125 g (4 oz) diced dried figs in the water in place of the dates. Make the sauce and puddings as above, adding 2 tablespoons chopped glacé ginger to the beaten pudding mix.

choco bread & butter pudding

Serves **4**

Preparation time **20 minutes**, plus standing

Cooking time **25 minutes**

4 **chocolate croissants**
50 g (2 oz) **unsalted butter**
50 g (2 oz) **caster sugar**
¼ teaspoon **ground mixed spice**
300 ml (½ pint) **milk**
4 **eggs**
1 teaspoon **vanilla essence**
icing sugar, to decorate

Grease a 1.2 litre (2 pint) shallow, round, ovenproof pie dish. Slice the croissants thickly and spread the butter over one side of each cut face of croissant. Stand the croissant slices upright and close together in the dish to completely fill it.

Mix the sugar and spice together, then spoon over the croissants and between the gaps. Stand the dish in a large roasting tin.

Beat the milk, eggs and vanilla essence together, then strain into the dish. Leave to stand for 15 minutes.

Pour hot water from the tap into the roasting tin to come halfway up the sides of the pie dish. Bake in a preheated oven, 180°C (350°F), Gas Mark 4, for about 25 minutes until the pudding is golden and the custard just set.

Lift the dish out of the roasting tin, dust with sifted icing sugar and serve the pudding warm with a little pouring cream.

For fruited bread & butter pudding, lightly butter 8 slices of white bread, cut into triangles and arrange in slightly overlapping layers in the dish, sprinkling with 75 g (3 oz) luxury dried fruit between the layers. Add the sugar as above, but omit the mixed spice. Mix the eggs, milk and vanilla, pour over the bread, then continue as above.

hot blackberry & apple trifle

Serves **4**
Preparation time **20 minutes**,
   plus cooling
Cooking time **20–25 minutes**

150 g (5 oz) **fresh** or **frozen**
   blackberries
2 **dessert apples**, cored,
   unpeeled and sliced
1 tablespoon **water**
50 g (2 oz) **caster sugar**
4 **trifle sponges**
3 tablespoons **dry** or **sweet**
   sherry
425 g (14 oz) can or carton
   custard

Meringue
3 **egg whites**
75 g (3 oz) **caster sugar**

Put the blackberries, apples, measured water and sugar in a saucepan, then cover and simmer for 5 minutes or until the fruit has softened. Leave the mixture to cool slightly.

Break the trifle sponges into chunks and arrange in an even layer in the base of a 1.2 litre (2 pint) ovenproof pie or soufflé dish and drizzle with the sherry. Spoon the poached fruit and syrup over the top, then cover with custard.

Whisk the egg whites in a large, dry bowl until stiffly peaking, then gradually whisk in the sugar, a teaspoonful at a time, until the meringue is stiff and glossy (see page 6). Spoon over the custard and swirl the top with the back of a spoon.

Bake in a preheated oven, 180°C (350°F), Gas Mark 4, for 15–20 minutes until heated through and the meringue is golden. Serve immediately.

For apple mallow, peel, core and thickly slice 8 dessert apples, then simmer in a saucepan with the grated rind and juice of 1 lemon, 4 cloves and 25 g (1 oz) caster sugar until tender. Spoon into a 1.2 litre (2 pint) ovenproof dish. Make the meringue as above, adding ¼ teaspoon ground cinnamon with the sugar. Spoon over the fruit, then bake as above. Serve the mallow warm.

vanilla soufflés & apricot coulis

Serves **8**
Preparation time **25 minutes**
Cooking time **25 minutes**

75 g (3 oz) **caster sugar**, plus
  extra for dusting
200 g (7 oz) **ready-to-eat
  dried apricots**, coarsely
  chopped
125 ml (4 fl oz) **water**, plus
  1 tablespoon
3 tablespoons **cornflour**
5 tablespoons **Cointreau** or
  other **orange-flavoured
  liqueur**
150 ml (¼ pint) **milk**
1 teaspoon **vanilla essence**
125 ml (4 fl oz) **double cream**
4 **eggs**, separated
icing sugar, for dusting

Grease 8 ramekin dishes and dust each one lightly with caster sugar. Put the apricots in a small pan with the measured water and simmer gently for 3 minutes until softened. Blend ½ teaspoon of the cornflour with 1 tablespoon water and add it to the pan. Cook gently for 1 minute or until the sauce has thickened.

Put the mixture in a food processor or blender, add the liqueur and blend until smooth. Divide the mixture among the ramekins.

Blend the remaining cornflour in a pan with a little of the milk. Add the remaining milk and heat gently, stirring, until thickened. Stir in 50 g (2 oz) of the caster sugar, the vanilla essence, cream and egg yolks and put in a large bowl.

Beat the egg whites until peaking and gradually beat in the remaining caster sugar. Using a large metal spoon, fold the egg whites into the custard.

Spoon the mixture into the ramekins and put them on a baking sheet. Bake in a preheated oven, 200°C (400°F), Gas Mark 6, for 20 minutes or until well risen. Dust with sifted icing sugar and serve immediately.

For apple & Calvados soufflés, peel, core and dice 4 dessert apples. Place in a small saucepan with 2 tablespoons water, cover and cook for 10 minutes until soft. Divide between 8 greased and sugared ramekins. Make the soufflés as above, adding 5 tablespoons Calvados or ordinary brandy instead of the Cointreau.

jam roly-poly

Serves **6**
Preparation time **25 minutes**
Cooking time **2 hours**

300 g (10 oz) **self-raising
    flour**
1 teaspoon **baking powder**
150 g (5 oz) **shredded
    vegetable suet**
75 g (3 oz) **caster sugar**
50 g (2 oz) **fresh
    breadcrumbs**
finely grated rind of 1 **lemon**
finely grated rind of 1 **orange**
1 **egg**, beaten
175–200 ml (6–7 fl oz) **milk**
6 tablespoons **raspberry jam**
150 g (5 oz) **frozen
    raspberries**, just defrosted

Put the flour, baking powder, suet and sugar in a bowl, then stir in the breadcrumbs and fruit rinds. Add the egg, then gradually mix in enough milk to make a soft but not sticky dough.

Knead lightly, then roll out to a 30 cm (12 inch) square. Spread with the jam, leaving a 2.5 cm (1 inch) border, then sprinkle the raspberries on top. Brush the border with a little milk, then roll up the pastry. Wrap loosely in a large piece of nonstick baking paper, twisting the edges together and leaving a little space for the pudding to rise, then wrap loosely in foil.

Put on a roasting rack set over a large roasting tin, then pour boiling water into the tin but not over the roasting rack. Cover the tin with foil and twist over the edges to seal well, then bake in a preheated oven, 150°C (300°F), Gas Mark 2, for 2 hours until the pudding is well risen. Check once or twice during baking and top up the water level if needed.

Transfer the pudding to a chopping board using a teacloth. Unwrap, cut into thick slices and serve with hot custard.

For spotted dick, warm 3 tablespoons orange juice or rum in a small saucepan, add 150 g (5 oz) raisins, 1 teaspoon ground ginger and ¼ teaspoon grated nutmeg and leave to soak for 1 hour or longer. Add to the flour mix just before adding the egg and milk. Shape into a long sausage, wrap in paper and foil and steam in the oven as above. Serve sliced with custard flavoured with a little extra rum, if liked.

double chocolate puddings

Serves **6**
Preparation time **25 minutes**
Cooking time **18–20 minutes**

125 g (4 oz) **unsalted butter**,
   at room temperature, or
   soft margarine
125 g (4 oz) **light muscovado**
   sugar
100 g (3½ oz) **self-raising**
   flour
15 g (½ oz) **cocoa powder**
2 **eggs**
75 g (3 oz) or 12 squares
   plain dark chocolate
100 g (3½ oz) **white**
   chocolate, broken into
   pieces
150 ml (¼ pint) **double cream**
¼ teaspoon **vanilla essence**

Put the butter or margarine, sugar, flour, cocoa and eggs into a mixing bowl or food processor and beat together until smooth. Divide the mixture between 6 greased sections of a deep muffin tin, then press 2 squares of dark chocolate into each and cover with the pudding mixture.

Bake in a preheated oven, 180°C (350°F), Gas Mark 4, for 18–20 minutes until well risen, slightly crusty around the edges and the centre springs back when pressed with a fingertip.

Meanwhile, warm the white chocolate, cream and vanilla essence together in a small saucepan, stirring until the chocolate has completely melted.

Loosen the edges of the baked puddings with a round-bladed knife, then turn out and transfer to shallow serving bowls. Drizzle with the white chocolate cream and serve immediately.

For walnut & chocolate puddings, omit the cocoa powder from the puddings and mix the butter, sugar and eggs with 125 g (4 oz) self-raising flour, 50 g (2 oz) roughly chopped walnuts and 2 level teaspoons instant coffee dissolved in 3 teaspoons boiling water. Spoon into the muffin tin and press the chocolate squares into the centre of each one as above. Bake as above and serve with pouring cream.

rice pudding with drunken raisins

Serves **4**

Preparation time **10 minutes**,
  plus soaking

Cooking time **2 hours**

50 g (2 oz) **raisins**

2 tablespoons **fortified wine**
  (such as **Pedro Ximénez**,
  Madeira or **sweet sherry**)

25 g (1 oz) **unsalted butter**,
  diced

65 g (2½ oz) **pudding rice**

25 g (1 oz) **caster sugar**

600 ml (1 pint) **milk**

large pinch of grated **nutmeg**
  and **cinnamon**

Put the raisins in a small saucepan with the fortified
wine and warm together, or microwave the raisins and
wine in a small bowl for 30 seconds on full power.
Leave to soak for 30 minutes or longer if time allows.

Grease a 900 ml (1½ pint) pie dish, then put in the
rice and the sugar. Spoon the soaked raisins on top,
then cover with the milk. Dot with the butter and
sprinkle with the spices.

Cook in a preheated oven, 150°C (300°F), Gas Mark
2, for 2 hours until the pudding is golden on top, the
rice is tender and the milk thick and creamy. Spoon into
bowls and serve with spoonfuls of extra-thick cream.

For traditional rice pudding, omit the raisins and
fortified wine and add the rice and sugar to the
greased pie dish. Pour over 450 ml (¾ pint) milk
and 150 ml (¼ pint) double cream. Dot with butter
as above, then sprinkle with just-grated nutmeg. Bake,
then serve with spoonfuls of strawberry jam.

chocolate & marshmallow torte

Serves **8**

Preparation time **40 minutes**, plus cooling

Cooking time **25–30 minutes**

200 g (7 oz) **plain dark chocolate**, broken into pieces

100 g (3½ oz) **unsalted butter**

5 **eggs**, separated

175 g (6 oz) **caster sugar**

2 tablespoons **plain flour**, sifted

½ teaspoon **ground cinnamon**

2 tablespoons **warm water**

300 ml (½ pint) **double cream**

125 g (4 oz) **mini pink and white marshmallows**

Put the chocolate and butter in a bowl set over a saucepan of gently simmering water and leave to melt.

Whisk the egg whites in a large bowl until stiff, moist-looking peaks are formed, then gradually whisk in half the sugar, a teaspoonful at a time, until thick and glossy (see page 6). Using the still dirty whisk, beat the egg yolks and remaining sugar in a third bowl until very thick.

Mix the warm chocolate and butter mixture gradually into the egg yolks. Stir in the flour and cinnamon, then loosen the mixture with the measured warm water. Gently fold in a spoonful of the meringue, then fold in the remainder.

Pour the mixture into a greased and base-lined 23 cm (9 inch) springform tin. Bake in a preheated oven, 180°C (350°F), Gas Mark 4, for 25–30 minutes until well risen and the top is crusty and the centre only just set. Leave to cool for 2 hours in the tin.

Remove the torte from the tin, discarding the lining paper. Cut into wedges. Softly whip the cream, then top wedges of torte with spoonfuls of cream and a sprinkling of marshmallows.

For mixed nut torte, fold in 100 g (3½ oz) mixed pistachios, hazelnuts and almonds, roughly chopped, after the flour and cinnamon. Serve with 4 tablespoons toasted flaked almonds instead of the marshmallows.

topsy-turvy banana gingercake

Serves **6**
Preparation time **25 minutes**
Cooking time **30 minutes**

4 tablespoons **golden syrup**,
  plus extra to serve
4 tablespoons **light**
  muscovado sugar
3 large **bananas**, halved
  lengthways
juice of 1 **lemon**

Gingercake
100 g (3½ oz) **unsalted butter**
100 g (3½ oz) **light**
  muscovado sugar
75 g (3 oz) **golden syrup**,
  plus extra for drizzling
2 **eggs**
4 tablespoons **milk**
175 g (6 oz) **wholemeal**
  plain flour
1 teaspoon **bicarbonate**
  of soda
2 teaspoons **ground ginger**

Grease a roasting tin with a base measurement of 23 x 18 cm (9 x 7 inches), and line the base with nonstick baking paper. Spoon the syrup and sugar into the base. Toss the bananas in the lemon juice, then arrange cut side downwards in the tin.

Heat the butter, sugar and syrup for the gingercake gently in a medium saucepan, stirring until melted. Take the pan off the heat.

Beat the eggs and milk in a jug, then mix the flour, bicarbonate of soda and ginger in a bowl. Gradually stir the milk mixture into the pan of melted butter, then stir in the flour mix and beat until smooth.

Pour the mixture over the bananas, then bake them in a preheated oven, 180°C (350°F), Gas Mark 4, for 30 minutes until well risen and the centre springs back when pressed.

Leave to cool for 5 minutes, then loosen the edge and invert the tin on to a large plate with a rim. Remove the tin and lining paper, then cut the pudding into portions. Serve drizzled with a little extra syrup or custard.

For homemade custard, to serve with the gingercake, beat 3 egg yolks with 3 tablespoons caster sugar and a few drops vanilla essence in a bowl. In a pan bring 300 ml (½ pint) milk just to the boil, then gradually mix into the yolks. Return to the pan. Heat gently, stirring continuously until the custard thickens and coats the back of the spoon (don't boil or the custard will curdle). If making in advance, sprinkle the surface with a little extra sugar to stop a skin forming.

pear & hazelnut sponge squares

Serves **6**
Preparation time **25 minutes**
Cooking time **25 minutes**

125 g (4 oz) **unsalted butter**,
  at room temperature, or
  soft margarine
125 g (4 oz) **caster sugar**
125 g (4 oz) **self-raising flour**
2 **eggs**
1 teaspoon **ground cinnamon**
75 g (3 oz) **hazelnuts**, roughly
  chopped
3 **pears**, quartered, cored
  and peeled and each piece
  halved again
icing sugar, for dusting

Blackberry sauce
250 g (8 oz) **blackberries**
25 g (1 oz) **caster sugar**
4 tablespoons **water**

Beat the butter or margarine, sugar, flour, eggs and cinnamon together in a bowl or combine in a food processor until smooth. Stir in 50 g (2 oz) of the hazelnuts. Grease a roasting tin with a base measurement of 23 x 18 cm (9 x 7 inches) and line the base with nonstick baking paper. Spoon the mixture into the tin and smooth into an even layer.

Arrange the pears randomly over the pudding mix, then sprinkle with the remaining hazelnuts. Bake in a preheated oven, 180°C (350°F), Gas Mark 4, for 25 minutes until golden brown and the sponge is well risen and springs back when pressed in the centre.

Cook 150 g (5 oz) of the blackberries in a saucepan with the sugar and water for 5 minutes until soft, then purée until smooth. Cut the sponge into portions, dust with sifted icing sugar and serve drizzled with the warm sauce, with the remaining blackberries.

For apple squares with chocolate sauce, omit the cinnamon and hazelnuts from the sponge mix, adding the grated rind of ½ orange instead. Spoon into the tin, then top with 3 cored, peeled and thickly sliced dessert apples and bake as above. Heat 4 tablespoons chocolate and hazelnut spread in a saucepan with 6 tablespoons milk to make a smooth chocolate sauce. Cut the sponge into squares, dust with sifted icing sugar and serve hot with the sauce.

apricot clafouti

Serves **4**

Preparation time **15 minutes,**
 plus standing

Cooking time **25 minutes**

50 g (2 oz) **plain flour**

2 tablespoons **caster sugar**

grated rind of ½ **lemon**

40 g (1½ oz) **unsalted butter**

1 **egg**

1 **egg yolk**

few drops **vanilla essence**

150 ml (¼ pint) mixed **milk**
 and **water**

410 g (13½ oz) can **apricot**
 halves, drained

icing sugar, for dusting

Sift the flour into a bowl and add the sugar and lemon rind. Melt 25 g (1 oz) of the butter, then add to the flour with the whole egg, egg yolk and vanilla essence. Gradually whisk in the milk and water until smooth. Leave to stand for 30 minutes or longer.

Grease liberally 4 individual 200 ml (7 fl oz) metal pudding moulds with the remaining butter. Quarter the apricots and divide among the tins. Stand the tins on a baking sheet, then cook in a preheated oven, 190°C (375°F), Gas Mark 5, for 5 minutes.

Pour the batter quickly into the pudding moulds so that the mix sizzles in the hot butter. Bake for about 20 minutes until well risen and golden brown. Dust the tops with sifted icing sugar and serve immediately, as the puddings sink as they cool.

For cherry clafouti, make the batter with the grated rind of ½ orange instead of the lemon. Drain a 350 g (11 oz) jar of morello cherries in syrup and divide the cherries between the pudding moulds as above. Bake the fruit and then add the batter as above.

orchard fruit crumble

Serves **6**
Preparation time **20 minutes**
Cooking time **30–35 minutes**

2 **dessert apples**
2 **pears**
400 g (13 oz) **red plums**,
   quartered and pitted
2 tablespoons **water**
75 g (3 oz) **caster sugar**
100 g (3½ oz) **plain flour**
50 g (2 oz) **unsalted butter**,
   diced
50 g (2 oz) **desiccated
   coconut**
50 g (2 oz) **milk chocolate
   chips**

Quarter, core and peel the apples and pears. Slice the quarters and add the slices to a 1.2 litre (2 pint) pie dish. Add the plums and the water, then sprinkle with 25 g (1 oz) of the sugar. Cover the dish with foil and bake in a preheated oven, 180°C (350°F), Gas Mark 4, for 10 minutes.

Put the remaining sugar in a bowl with the flour and butter, then rub the butter in with your fingertips or an electric mixer until the mixture resembles fine crumbs. Stir in the coconut and chocolate chips.

Remove the foil from the fruit and spoon the crumble over the top. Bake for 20–25 minutes until golden brown and the fruit is tender. Serve warm with custard or cream.

For plum & orange crumble, put 750 g (1½ lb) plums, quartered and pitted, into a 1.2 litre (2 pint) pie dish with 50 g (2 oz) caster sugar. Make the crumble as above, adding the grated rind of 1 small orange and 50 g (2 oz) ground almonds instead of the coconut and chocolate chips. Bake as above.

toffee & banana pancakes

Serves **4**
Preparation time **15 minutes**,
   plus resting
Cooking time **30 minutes**

100 g (3½ oz) **plain flour**
pinch **salt**
1 egg
1 egg yolk
300 ml (½ pint) **milk**
2–3 tablespoons **sunflower
   oil**
2 **bananas**, sliced

Toffee sauce
50 g (2 oz) **unsalted butter**
50 g (2 oz) **light muscovado
   sugar**
2 tablespoons **golden syrup**
150 ml (¼ pint) **double cream**

Sift the flour into a bowl, add the salt, egg and egg
yolk, then gradually whisk in the milk to make a smooth
batter. Set aside for 30 minutes.

Put the butter, sugar and syrup for the toffee sauce in
a small saucepan and heat gently, stirring occasionally,
until the butter has melted and the sugar dissolved.
Bring to the boil and cook for 3–4 minutes until just
beginning to darken around the edges.

Take the pan off the heat, then gradually pour in the
cream. Tilt the pan to mix and as bubbles subside stir
with a wooden spoon. Set aside.

Pour the oil for cooking the pancakes into an 18 cm
(7 inch) frying pan, heat and then pour off the excess
into a small bowl or jug. Pour a little pancake batter
over the base of the pan, tilt the pan to coat the base
evenly with batter, then cook for 2 minutes until the
underside is golden. Loosen with a palette knife, turn
over and cook the second side in the same way. When
cooked, slide on to a plate and keep hot. Cook the
remaining batter, oiling the pan as needed.

Fold the pancakes and arrange on serving plates. Top
with banana slices and drizzle with the toffee sauce.

For citrus pancakes, make the pancakes as above,
then drizzle them with the freshly squeezed juice
of 1 lemon and 1 orange. Sprinkle with 50 g (2 oz)
caster sugar before serving.

cranberry eve's pudding

Serves **6**

Preparation time **25 minutes**

Cooking time **40–50 minutes**

750 g (1½ lb) **cooking apples**, quartered, cored, peeled and thickly sliced

125 g (4 oz) **frozen cranberries**

75 g (3 oz) **caster sugar**

1 tablespoon **water**

icing sugar, for dusting

Topping

125 g (4 oz) **unsalted butter**, at room temperature, or **soft margarine**

125 g (4 oz) **caster sugar**

125 g (4 oz) **self-raising flour**

2 **eggs**

grated rind of 1 small **orange**, plus 2 tablespoons of the juice

Put the apples and cranberries into a 1.5 litre (2½ pint), 5 cm (2 inch) deep ovenproof dish and sprinkle over the sugar and water. Cook, uncovered, in a preheated oven, 180°C (350°F), Gas Mark 4, for 10 minutes.

Put the butter, sugar, flour and eggs for the topping in a bowl, and beat together until smooth. Stir in the orange rind and juice.

Spoon the mixture over the partially cooked fruit and spread into an even layer. Return to the oven and cook for 30–40 minutes until the topping is golden and the centre springs back when pressed with a fingertip. Dust with sifted icing sugar and serve warm with custard or cream.

For apple & blackberry pudding, omit the cranberries and add 125 g (4 oz) frozen blackberries. Make the topping as above, but add the grated rind of 1 lemon and 2 tablespoons of the juice instead of the orange rind and juice.

gingered profiteroles

Serves **4**
Preparation time **35 minutes**, plus cooling
Cooking time **20 minutes**

150 ml (¼ pint) **water**
50 g (2 oz) **unsalted butter**
pinch **salt**
65 g (2½ oz) **plain flour**, sifted
2 **eggs**
½ teaspoon **vanilla essence**
250 ml (8 fl oz) **double cream**
50 g (2 oz) **crystallized** or
  glacé ginger, finely chopped

Sauce
150 g (5 oz) **plain dark
  chocolate**, broken into
  pieces
150 ml (¼ pint) **milk**
50 g (2 oz) **caster sugar**
2 tablespoons **brandy**

Pour the measured water into a medium saucepan, add the butter and salt and heat until the butter has melted. Bring up to the boil, then take off the heat and stir in the flour. Put the pan back on the heat and cook briefly, stirring until the mixture makes a smooth ball. Leave to cool.

Beat the eggs and vanilla essence together, then gradually beat into the flour mixture until smooth. Spoon the mixture into a large piping bag fitted with a 1.5 cm (¾ inch) plain piping tube. Lightly grease a large baking sheet then pipe on 20 balls, leaving space between them.

Bake in a preheated oven, 200°C (400°F), Gas Mark 6, for 15 minutes until well risen. Make a slit in the side of each ball for the steam to escape, return to the turned-off oven for 5 minutes, then take out and cool.

Make the sauce by heating the chocolate, milk and sugar in a saucepan and stirring until smooth. Take off the heat and mix in the brandy.

Whip the cream until it forms soft swirls, fold in the ginger, then enlarge the slit in each profiterole and spoon in the ginger cream. Pile into serving dishes and drizzle with reheated sauce.

For Black Forest puffs, drain and chop a 425 g (14 oz) can of black cherries in juice. Fold into the whipped cream instead of the ginger, then fill the profiteroles as above. Omit the brandy from the sauce, adding 2 tablespoons kirsch instead.

peach & blueberry jalousie

Serves **6**
Preparation time **30 minutes**
Cooking time **20–25 minutes**

500 g (1 lb) chilled **ready-
   made puff pastry** or
   homemade flaky pastry
   (see page 7)
a little **flour**, for dusting
4 ripe **peaches** or **nectarines**,
   thickly sliced
125 g (4 oz) **blueberries**
50 g (2 oz) **caster sugar**, plus
   a little extra to decorate
grated rind of ½ **lemon**
1 **egg**, beaten
icing sugar, for dusting

Roll out half the pastry on a lightly floured surface and trim to a 30 x 18 cm (12 x 7 inch) rectangle. Transfer to a lightly greased baking sheet.

Pile the peach or nectarine slices on top, leaving a 2.5 cm (1 inch) border of pastry showing, then sprinkle on the blueberries, sugar and lemon rind. Brush the pastry border with a little beaten egg.

Roll out the remaining pastry to a little larger than the first piece, then trim to 33 x 20 cm (13 x 8 inches). Fold in half lengthways, then make cuts in from the fold about 1 cm (½ inch) apart and about 6 cm (2½ inches) long, leaving a wide uncut border of pastry.

Lift the pastry over the fruit, unfold so that the fruit and bottom layer of pastry are completely covered, then press the pastry edges together. Trim if needed. Knock up the edges with a knife, then flute the edges by pressing the first and second finger on to the pie edge, then make small cuts with a knife between them to create a scalloped edge.

Brush the top of the pastry with beaten egg, sprinkle with a little extra sugar and bake in a preheated oven, 200°C (400°F), Gas Mark 6, for 20–25 minutes until the pastry is well risen and golden brown. Serve cut into squares, warm or cold, with cream or ice cream.

For apple & blackberry jalousie, replace the peaches and blueberries with 4 Granny Smith apples, cored, quartered and thickly sliced, and 125 g (4 oz) blackberries.

freeform apple & mixed berry pie

Serves **6**

Preparation time **30 minutes**, plus chilling

Cooking time **20–25 minutes**

275 g (9 oz) **plain flour**, plus extra for dusting

75 g (3 oz) **icing sugar**

125 g (4 oz) **unsalted butter**, at room temperature, diced

2 **eggs**

a little **milk** or beaten **egg**, to glaze

caster sugar, to decorate

Filling

2 **cooking apples**, about 500 g (1 lb), cored, peeled and thickly sliced

175 g (6 oz) **frozen mixed berries** (no need to defrost)

50 g (2 oz) **icing sugar**

2 teaspoons **cornflour**

Put the flour on a large board or straight on to the work surface, add the icing sugar and butter, then make a dip in the centre and add the eggs. Begin to mix the eggs and butter together with your fingertips, gradually drawing the flour and sugar into the mix until it begins to clump together and you can squeeze the pastry into a ball. Knead the pastry lightly, then chill in the refrigerator for 15 minutes.

Mix together the apples, frozen mixed berries, icing sugar and cornflour for the filling.

Roll out the pastry on a lightly floured surface until it forms a rough-shaped circle about 33 cm (13 inches) in diameter. Lift it over a rolling pin on to a large greased baking sheet. Pile the fruit mix high in the centre of the pastry, then bring the edges of the pastry up and around the fruit, shaping into soft pleats and leaving the centre of the fruit mound exposed.

Brush the outside of the pie with a little milk or beaten egg and sprinkle with caster sugar. Bake in a preheated oven, 190°C (375°F), Gas Mark 5, for 20–25 minutes until the pastry is golden and the fruit tender. Serve warm or cold with custard or cream.

For spiced plum & peach pie, replace the apples and berries with 400 g (13 oz) ripe red plums, pitted and sliced, and 2 ripe peaches, sliced. Mix with the sugar and cornflour as above, adding ½ teaspoon ground cinnamon. Make the pie and bake as above.

portuguese custard tarts

Makes **12**
Preparation time **25 minutes**,
  plus cooling
Cooking time **35 minutes**

1 tablespoon **vanilla sugar**
½ teaspoon **ground cinnamon**
450 g (14½ oz) chilled **ready-
  made** or **homemade sweet
  shortcrust pastry** (see
  page 7)
a little **flour**, for dusting
3 **eggs**
2 **egg yolks**
2 tablespoons **caster sugar**
1 teaspoon **vanilla essence**
300 ml (½ pint) **double cream**
150 ml (¼ pint) **milk**
icing sugar, for dusting

Mix the vanilla sugar with the cinnamon. Cut the pastry
in half and roll out each piece on a lightly floured
surface to a 20 cm (8 inch) square. Sprinkle 1 square
with the spiced sugar and position the second square
on top. Reroll the pastry to a 40 x 30 cm (16 x 12 inch)
rectangle and cut out 12 circles, each 10 cm (4 inch)
across, using a large cutter or small bowl as a guide.

Press the pastry circles into the sections of a 12-hole
nonstick muffin tray, pressing them firmly into the
bottom and around the sides. Prick each pastry base,
line with a square of foil, add macaroni or beans and
bake blind (see pages 6–7) in a preheated oven,
190°C (375°F), Gas Mark 5, for 10 minutes. Remove
the foil and macaroni or beans and bake for an
additional 5 minutes. Reduce the oven temperature to
160°C (325°F), Gas Mark 3.

Beat together the eggs, egg yolks, caster sugar and
vanilla essence. Heat the cream and milk in a pan until
bubbling around the edges and pour it over the egg
mixture, stirring. Strain the custard into a jug and pour
into the pastry shells.

Bake for about 20 minutes or until the custard is only
just set. Let the tarts cool in the tin, then remove and
serve dusted with icing sugar.

For French prune custard tarts, put 12 ready-to-eat
pitted prunes in the base of each blind-baked pastry
case, then pour the custard over and bake as above.
Serve warm with spoonfuls of crème fraîche.

gateau pithiviers with plums

Serves **6**
Preparation time **30 minutes**
Cooking time **25–30 minutes**

100 g (3½ oz) **unsalted
  butter**, at room temperature
100 g (3½ oz) **caster sugar**
100 g (3½ oz) **ground
  almonds**
few drops **almond essence**
1 **egg**, beaten, plus extra for
  glazing
500 g (1 lb) chilled **ready-
  made puff pastry** or
  homemade flaky pastry
  (see page 7)
a little **flour**, for dusting
375 g (12 oz) **plums**, pitted
  and thickly sliced
icing sugar, for dusting

Cream the butter and sugar together in a bowl until pale and smooth. Add the almonds and almond essence, then the egg, and mix together until smooth.

Roll out half the pastry thinly on a lightly floured surface and trim to a 25 cm (10 inch) circle using a dinner plate as a guide. Place on a wetted baking sheet, then spread the almond paste over the top leaving a 2.5 cm (1 inch) border of pastry around the edges. Arrange the plums in a single layer on top. Brush the pastry border with a little beaten egg.

Roll out the remaining pastry thinly and trim to a circle a little larger than the first. Cut 5 or 6 swirly 'S' shapes out of the centre of the pastry, then lift over a rolling pin and position on the almond paste. Press the edges together to seal, and trim to neaten if needed. Knock up the edge to separate the pastry layers slightly, then flute the edge (see page 42).

Brush the top with beaten egg and bake in a preheated oven, 200°C (400°F), Gas Mark 6, for 25–30 minutes until well risen and golden.

Leave to cool slightly, then dust the top with icing sugar and serve cut into wedges with cream.

For brandied prune Pithiviers, soak 150 g (5 oz) ready-to-eat pitted prunes in 3 tablespoons brandy, then arrange over the almond paste instead of the plums. Continue as above.

cherry frangipane tart

Serves **8**
Preparation time **35 minutes**,
 plus chilling and cooling
Cooking time **50 minutes**

450 g (14½ oz) chilled **ready-
 made** or **homemade sweet
 shortcrust pastry** (see
 page 7)
a little **flour**, for dusting
250 g (8 oz) **fresh cherries**,
 pitted, or a 425 g (14 oz)
 can, drained
3 **eggs**
100 g (3½ oz) **caster sugar**
75 g (3 oz) **unsalted butter**,
 melted
few drops **almond essence**
100 g (3½ oz) **ground
 almonds**
2 tablespoons **flaked
 almonds**
icing sugar, for dusting

Roll out the pastry on a lightly floured surface until
large enough to line a 25 cm (10 inch) greased deep-
fluted, loose-bottomed flan tin. Lift the pastry over a
rolling pin, then press it over the base and sides of the
tin. Trim the top, then chill for 15 minutes.

Prick the base of the tart with a fork. Line the pastry
with nonstick baking paper, add macaroni or beans
and bake blind (see pages 6–7) in a preheated oven,
190°C (375°F), Gas Mark 5, for 15 minutes. Remove
the paper and macaroni or beans and cook for a
further 5 minutes.

Arrange the cherries in the base of the tart. Whisk
the eggs and sugar together until thick and the whisk
leaves a trail when lifted out of the mixture. Gently fold
in the melted butter and almond essence, then the
ground almonds. Pour the mixture over the cherries
and sprinkle with the flaked almonds.

Reduce the oven to 180°C (350°F), Gas Mark 4, and
cook the tart for 30 minutes until golden brown and
the filling is set. Check after 20 minutes and cover the
top loosely with foil if the tart appears to be browning
too quickly.

Leave to cool in the tin for 30 minutes, then remove
and dust with sifted icing sugar before serving.

For Bakewell tart, make the tart case and bake blind
as above, then spread 4 tablespoons strawberry or
raspberry jam over the base. Add the almond mixture
and flaked almonds and bake as above.

pear & almond tart

Serves **8**

Preparation time **20 minutes**, plus chilling

Cooking time **50–55 minutes**

450 g (14½ oz) chilled **ready-made** or **homemade sweet shortcrust pastry** (see page 7)

a little **flour**, for dusting

125 g (4 oz) **unsalted butter**, softened

125 g (4 oz) **caster sugar**

125 g (4 oz) **ground almonds**

2 **eggs**, lightly beaten

1 tablespoon **lemon juice**

3 ripe **pears**, peeled, cored and thickly sliced

25 g (1 oz) **flaked almonds**

icing sugar, for dusting

Roll out the pastry on a lightly floured surface and use it to line a 25 cm (10 inch) flan tin. Prick the base with a fork and chill for 30 minutes. Line with nonstick baking paper, add macaroni or beans and bake blind (see pages 6–7) in a preheated oven, 190°C (375°F), Gas Mark 5, for 15 minutes. Remove the baking paper and macaroni or beans and bake for a further 5–10 minutes until the pastry is crisp and golden. Leave to cool completely. Reduce the temperature to 190°C (375°F), Gas Mark 5.

Beat the butter, sugar and ground almonds together until smooth, then beat in the eggs and lemon juice.

Arrange the pear slices over the pastry case and carefully spread over the almond mixture. Sprinkle with the flaked almonds and bake for 30 minutes until the topping is golden and firm to the touch. Remove from the oven and leave to cool.

Dust the tart with sifted icing sugar and serve in wedges with chocolate sauce (see below) and some vanilla ice cream.

For chocolate sauce, to serve as an accompaniment, melt 100 g (3½ oz) plain dark chocolate, chopped, 50 g (2 oz) unsalted butter, diced, and 1 tablespoon golden syrup together. Leave to cool slightly.

sweet fruity pizzas

Serves **4**
Preparation time **25 minutes**,
  plus rising
Cooking time **12–15 minutes**

250 g (8 oz) **strong white
  flour**, plus extra for dusting
¼ teaspoon **salt**
2 tablespoons **caster sugar**
¾ teaspoon **fast-action dried
  yeast**
2 tablespoons **olive oil**
150 ml (¼ pint) **warm water**

Topping
150 g (5 oz) **full-fat
  mascarpone cheese**
2 tablespoons **icing sugar**
½ teaspoon **vanilla essence**
2 **peaches**, pitted and sliced
2 **figs**, quartered
125 g (4 oz) **fresh
  raspberries**
2 tablespoons **maple syrup**,
  plus extra to serve

Put the flour, salt, sugar and yeast in a bowl and mix together. Add the oil, then gradually stir in the measured warm water and mix to a smooth dough. Knead on a lightly floured surface for 5 minutes until smooth and elastic. Put back in the bowl, cover with greased clingfilm and leave in a warm place for about 45 minutes until doubled in size.

Knead the dough for a second time, then roll out to 4 rough-shaped circles about 18 cm (7 inches) in diameter. Place on 2 greased baking sheets.

Mix the mascarpone with the icing sugar and vanilla essence, then spread over the pizzas leaving a rim of dough. Arrange the fruit on top. Leave to rise for 15 minutes. Drizzle with the maple syrup, then bake in a preheated oven, 200°C (400°F), Gas Mark 6, for 12–15 minutes until the pizzas are golden and the bread bases cooked through.

Leave to stand for 5 minutes, drizzle with a little extra maple syrup, then serve.

For marzipan & nectarine fruit kuchen, add the grated rind of 1 lemon when mixing the bread dough, knead, leave to rise and knead again as above, then press into a 25 cm (10 inch) greased fluted, loose-bottomed flan tin. Sprinkle with 75 g (3 oz) grated marzipan, then arrange 2 sliced nectarines over the top. Drizzle with 2 tablespoons melted butter and 2 tablespoons caster sugar. Leave to rise, then bake for 25–30 minutes at the temperature given above, covering with foil after 15 minutes if overbrowning.

mixed berry tartlets

Serves **6**
Preparation time **20 minutes**, plus chilling
Cooking time **40–48 minutes**

450 g (14½ oz) chilled **ready-made** or **homemade sweet shortcrust pastry** (see page 7)
a little **flour**, for dusting
icing sugar, for dusting

Filling
125 g (4 oz) **unsalted butter**, softened
125 g (4 oz) **caster sugar**
2 **eggs**, lightly beaten
125 g (4 oz) **ground hazelnuts**
175 g (6 oz) **mixed summer berries** (such as raspberries and blueberries)

Apricot glaze
250 g (8 oz) **apricot jam**
2 teaspoons **lemon juice**
2 teaspoons **water**

Divide the pastry into 3 pieces and roll each one out thinly on a lightly floured surface. Use to line 3 x 12 cm (5 inch) fluted flan tins. Prick the bases with a fork and chill for 30 minutes. Line with nonstick baking paper, add macaroni or beans and bake blind (see pages 6–7) in a preheated oven, 190°C (375°F), Gas Mark 5, for 10 minutes. Remove the paper and macaroni or beans and bake for a further 5–8 minutes until crisp and golden. Leave to cool. Reduce the temperature to 180°C (350°F), Gas Mark 4.

Beat the butter and sugar until pale and light, then gradually beat in the eggs. Fold in the hazelnuts.

Divide the berries among the pastry cases and spoon over the hazelnut mixture, spreading it flat. Bake for 25–30 minutes or until risen and firm to the touch.

Put the jam in a small pan with the lemon juice and measured water and heat gently until the jam melts. Increase the heat and boil for 1 minute, remove from the heat and press through a fine sieve. Keep warm.

Brush the warm apricot glaze brush over the tarts as soon as they come out of the oven. Leave to cool in the tins and serve dusted with icing sugar.

For raspberry & almondine tart, line a 20 cm (8 inch) flan tin with pastry and bake blind as above. Sprinkle over 175 g (6 oz) fresh raspberries. Cream the butter and sugar as above, then beat in the eggs, 125 g (4 oz) ground almonds and a few drops almond essence. Spoon into the case and sprinkle with 3 tablespoons flaked almonds. Bake as above for 35–45 minutes.

deep dish puff apple pie

Serves **6**
Preparation time **40 minutes**,
  plus chilling
Cooking time **20–25 minutes**

1 kg (2 lb) or about 5 **cooking
  apples**, quartered, cored,
  peeled and thickly sliced
100 g (3½ oz) **caster sugar**,
  plus extra for sprinkling
grated rind of 1 small **orange**
½ teaspoon **ground mixed
  spice** or **ground cinnamon**
3 whole **cloves**
400 g (13 oz) chilled **ready-
  made puff pastry** or
  homemade flaky pastry
  (see page 7)
a little **flour**, for dusting
1 **egg**, beaten

Fill a 1.2 litre (2 pint) pie dish with the apples. Mix
the sugar with the orange rind, mixed spice and cloves,
then sprinkle over the apples.

Roll the pastry out on a lightly floured surface until a
little larger than the top of the dish. Cut 2 long strips
from the edges, about 1 cm (½ inch) wide. Brush the
dish rim with a little beaten egg, press the strips on top,
then brush these with egg. Lift the remaining pastry
over the dish and press the edges together well.

Trim off the excess pastry, knock up the edges with a
small knife, then flute. Reroll the trimmings and cut out
small heart shapes or circles with a small biscuit cutter.
Brush the top of the pie with beaten egg, add pastry
shapes, then brush these with egg. Sprinkle with a little
extra sugar.

Bake in a preheated oven, 200°C (400°F), Gas Mark
6, for 20–25 minutes until the pastry is well risen and
golden. Serve warm with spoonfuls of crème fraîche or
extra-thick cream.

For spiced plum & pear pie, substitute 500 g (1 lb)
sliced pears and 500 g (1 lb) sliced plums for the
apples, sprinkle with 75 g (3 oz) caster sugar and add
2 halved star anise, 3 cloves and ¼ teaspoon ground
cinnamon. Omit the fruit rind, then cover with the
pastry and continue as above.

mango & palm sugar tatin

Serves **8**

Preparation time **40 minutes**, plus freezing

Cooking time **20–25 minutes**

75 g (3 oz) **unsalted butter**

75 g (3 oz) **palm sugar**, grated, or **light soft brown sugar**

½ teaspoon ground **mixed spice**

3 small **mangoes**, peeled, pitted and thickly sliced

350 g (12 oz) chilled **ready-made puff pastry** or **homemade flaky pastry** (see page 7)

a little **flour**, for dusting

Make the topping. Heat the butter, sugar and spice together in a 23 cm (9 inch) ovenproof frying pan until the butter has melted. Remove the pan from the heat. Carefully arrange the mango slices in the pan, fanning them from the centre outwards, to make 2 layers.

Roll out the pastry on a lightly floured surface and trim to a round a little larger than the size of the pan. Press it down over the mangoes and into the edges of the pan and pierce a small hole in the centre. Bake in a preheated oven, 220°C (425°F), Gas Mark 7, for 20–25 minutes until the pastry is risen and golden. Leave to stand for 10 minutes before turning out on to a large plate. Serve with ice cream.

For coconut ice cream, to accompany the tatin, bring 300 ml (½ pint) full-fat milk, 400 ml (14 fl oz) can full-fat coconut milk and 2 star anise just to the boil in a saucepan. Take off the heat and leave to infuse for 20 minutes, then strain. Beat 5 egg yolks with 75 g (3 oz) caster sugar until pale and creamy. Stir in the cream mix, then pour back into the pan and heat gently, stirring until it coats the back of the spoon. Cool, then freeze in an electric ice-cream machine until thick or in a plastic box in the freezer, beating several times until firm.

kaffir lime tart

Serves **8**
Preparation time **20 minutes**, plus chilling
Cooking time **33–40 minutes**

400 g (13 oz) chilled **ready-made** or **homemade sweet shortcrust pastry** (see page 7)
a little **flour**, for dusting
175 g (6 oz) **caster sugar**
200 ml (7 fl oz) freshly squeezed **lime juice** (4–6 limes)
8 **kaffir lime leaves** or the grated rind of 3 **limes**
3 **eggs**
2 **egg yolks**
175 g (6 oz) **unsalted butter**, softened
icing sugar, for dusting

Roll out the pastry on a lightly floured surface and use it to line a 23 cm (9 inch) flan tin. Prick the base with a fork and chill for 30 minutes. Line with nonstick baking paper, add macaroni or beans and bake blind (see pages 6–7) in a preheated oven, 200°C (400°F), Gas Mark 6, for 15 minutes. Remove the paper and macaroni or beans and bake for a further 12–15 minutes until the pastry is crisp and golden. Set aside to cool.

Make the filling. Put the sugar, lime juice and kaffir lime leaves or lime rind in a saucepan and heat gently to dissolve the sugar. Bring to the boil and simmer for 5 minutes. Leave to cool for 5 minutes, then strain into a clean pan.

Stir in the eggs, egg yolks and half the butter and heat gently, stirring, for 1 minute or until the sauce coats the back of the spoon. Add the remaining butter and whisk constantly until the mixture thickens.

Transfer the lime mixture to the pastry case and bake for 6–8 minutes until set. Leave to cool and serve warm dusted with icing sugar.

For mango & kiwifruit salad, to serve with the tart, peel, stone and dice 1 large mango, then mix with 3 peeled and sliced kiwifruits, the seeds scooped from 3 passion fruits and the juice of 1 lime.

plum tripiti

Makes **24**
Preparation time **40 minutes**
Cooking time **10 minutes**

100 g (3½ oz) **feta cheese**,
   drained and coarsely grated
100 g (3½ oz) **ricotta cheese**
50 g (2 oz) **caster sugar**
¼ teaspoon **ground cinnamon**
1 **egg**, beaten
75 g (3 oz) **unsalted butter**
12 sheets chilled **filo pastry**
   from a 200 g (7 oz) pack
a little **flour**, for dusting
500 g (1 lb) small red **plums**,
   halved and pitted
icing sugar, for dusting

Mix the feta, ricotta, sugar, cinnamon and egg in a bowl. Melt the butter in a small saucepan.

Unfold the pastry sheets on a lightly floured surface, then put one in front of you, with a short side facing you. Cover the remaining sheets with clingfilm to prevent them drying out. Brush the pastry sheet with a little of the melted butter, then cut in half to make two long strips. Place a spoonful of the cheese mixture a little up from the bottom left-hand corner of each strip, then cover with a plum half. Fold the bottom right-hand corner of one strip diagonally over the plum to cover the filling and to make a triangle.

Fold the bottom left-hand corner upwards to make a second triangle, then keep folding until the top of the strip is reached and the filling is enclosed in a triangle of pastry. Place on a baking sheet and repeat until 24 triangles have been made using all the filling.

Brush the outside of the triangles with the remaining butter and cook in a preheated oven, 200°C (400°F), Gas Mark 6, for about 10 minutes until the pastry is golden and the plum juices begin to run from the sides. Dust with a little sifted icing sugar and leave to cool for 15 minutes before serving.

For gingered peach tripiti, make the filling in the same way but flavour with 2 tablespoons finely chopped glacé or stem ginger instead of ground cinnamon. Top with 2 ripe peaches, each cut into 12 pieces.

apple & muscatel strudel

Serves **6**

Preparation time **30 minutes**, plus soaking

Cooking time **30–35 minutes**

100 g (3½ oz) **muscatel raisins**

2 tablespoons **brandy**

750 g (1½ lb) **dessert apples**, quartered, cored and cut into small dice

75 g (3 oz) **fresh white breadcrumbs**

50 g (2 oz) **soft light brown sugar**

grated rind of 1 **lemon**

50 g (2 oz) **pine nuts**, toasted

1 teaspoon **ground cinnamon**, plus extra for dusting

12 sheets chilled **filo pastry** from a 200 g (7 oz) pack

a little **flour**, for dusting

65 g (2½ oz) **unsalted butter**, melted

2 tablespoons **icing sugar**, for dusting

Put the raisins in a bowl and cover with the brandy. Set aside to soak for 2 hours.

Put the apples in a bowl and add the breadcrumbs, sugar, lemon rind, pine nuts, cinnamon and the raisins and their juices. Stir well.

Lay 2 sheets of the pastry on a lightly floured work surface, next to each other and overlapping by about 2.5 cm (1 inch) to form a larger sheet of pastry. Brush with melted butter, then top with the remaining pastry, brushing each layer with a little butter.

Spread the apple mixture over the pastry, leaving a 5 cm (2 inch) border. Fold the long sides over the filling. Brush with butter and roll up from a short side to form a Swiss roll.

Transfer to a baking sheet, brush with the remaining melted butter and bake in a preheated oven, 200°C (400°F), Gas Mark 6, for 30–35 minutes until lightly golden. Combine the sifted icing sugar with a little extra cinnamon and dust the strudel. Serve hot with custard or whipped cream.

For plum & almond strudel, omit the raisins, brandy and apples and mix 625 g (1¼ lb) pitted and thickly sliced red plums with the breadcrumbs, sugar, lemon rind, 50 g (2 oz) ground almonds and 1 teaspoon ground cinnamon. Continue as above.

white chocolate & raspberry puffs

Serves **6**

Preparation time **20 minutes**, plus chilling

Cooking time **15 minutes**

375 g (12 oz) chilled **ready-made puff pastry** or **homemade flaky pastry** (see page 7)

a little **flour**, for dusting

200 ml (7 fl oz) **double cream**

½ **vanilla pod**

200 g (7 oz) **white chocolate**, chopped

150 g (5 oz) **raspberries**

icing sugar, for dusting

Roll out the pastry dough on a lightly floured surface until it is a rectangle 2.5 mm (⅛ inch) thick. Cut it into 6 rectangles, each 12 x 7 cm (5 x 3 inches), and put them on a baking sheet. Chill for 30 minutes. Bake in a preheated oven, 200°C (400°F), Gas Mark 6, for 15 minutes until the pastry is puffed and golden. Transfer to a wire rack to cool.

Put the cream and vanilla pod in a saucepan and heat gently until it reaches boiling point. Remove from the heat and scrape the seeds from the vanilla pod into the cream (discard the pod). Immediately stir in the chocolate and continue stirring until it has melted. Cool, chill for 1 hour until firm, then whisk until spreadable.

Split the pastries in half crossways and fill each with white chocolate cream and raspberries. Serve dusted with sifted icing sugar.

For strawberry custard creams, make the pastry rectangles as above, then cool. Whip 150 ml (¼ pint) double cream until it forms soft swirls, then fold in a 125 g (4 oz) tub of ready-made custard. Split and fill the pastries with custard cream and 250 g (8 oz) sliced strawberries. Dust the tops with sifted icing sugar before serving.

banoffee pie

Serves **6**
Preparation time **35 minutes**,
    plus chilling and cooling
Cooking time **8 minutes**

200 g (7 oz) **unsalted butter**
2 tablespoons **golden syrup**
250 g (8 oz) **digestive
    biscuits**, crushed
100 g (3½ oz) **dark
    muscovado sugar**
400 g (13 oz) can **full-fat
    condensed milk**
300 ml (½ pint) **double cream**
3 small **bananas**
juice of 1 **lemon**
plain dark chocolate, grated,
    to decorate

Melt half the butter and the syrup in a saucepan, add the biscuit crumbs and mix well. Tip into a greased 20 cm (8 inch) springform tin and press evenly over the base and up the sides almost to the tin's top. Chill.

Heat the remaining butter and the sugar in a nonstick frying pan until the butter has melted and the sugar dissolved. Add the condensed milk and cook over a medium heat, stirring continuously, for 4–5 minutes until the mixture thickens and it begins to smell of caramel (don't have the heat too high or the condensed milk will burn).

Take the pan off the heat and leave the mixture to cool for 1–2 minutes, then pour into the biscuit case. Allow to cool completely, then chill for at least 1 hour.

Whip the cream until it forms soft peaks just before serving. Halve the bananas lengthways, then slice them and toss them in the lemon juice. Fold two-thirds into the cream, then spoon over the toffee layer. Arrange the remaining bananas on top. Loosen the edge of the biscuit crust with a palette knife, then remove the tin and transfer the pie to a serving plate. Sprinkle with grated chocolate and serve cut into wedges.

For banoffee ice cream sundae, make the toffee sauce as above but cook for just 2 minutes so that it is runnier, then leave to cool. Layer the sliced bananas in 6 glasses with 12 scoops vanilla ice cream, 6 crumbled brandy snap biscuits and a drizzle of the sauce, reheated if very thick. Sprinkle the top with chocolate curls or grated chocolate.

papaya, lime & mango tartlets

Makes **20**
Preparation time **35 minutes**
Cooking time **15–20 minutes**

250 g (8 oz) chilled **ready-
made** or **homemade sweet
shortcrust pastry** (see
page 7)
a little **flour**, for dusting
thinly grated rind and juice of
2 large, juicy **limes**
6 tablespoons **double cream**
150 ml (¼ pint) **full-fat
condensed milk**
2 tablespoons finely diced
papaya
2 tablespoons finely diced
mango
lime rind, to decorate

Roll out the pastry on a lightly floured surface to a
2.5 mm (⅛ inch) thickness, then, using a 5 cm (2 inch)
round biscuit or pastry cutter, stamp out 20 rounds.
Use the pastry rounds to line 20 x 5 cm (2 inch) mini
tartlet tins. Prick the pastry bases with a fork. Line with
nonstick baking paper, add macaroni or beans and
bake blind (see pages 6–7) in a preheated oven,
190°C (375°F), Gas Mark 5, for 10 minutes, then
remove the paper and macaroni or beans and return
the cases to the oven for 5–10 minutes or until they
are crisp and golden. Remove from the oven.

Put the lime rind in a blender with the cream and
condensed milk and pulse until well combined. With
the motor running, slowly pour in the lime juice and
process until blended. (Alternatively, mix well by hand.)
Transfer to a bowl, cover and chill in the refrigerator for
3–4 hours or until firm.

Put the cases on a serving platter and spoon the lime
mixture into each case. Mix the mango with the papaya
and, using a teaspoon, top the cases. Decorate with
lime rind and serve immediately.

For summer berry tartlets, make the pastry cases
and filling as above. Spoon the filling into the cases.
Warm 3 tablespoons redcurrant jelly with the grated
rind and juice of 1 lime, cook until syrupy, then stir in
150 g (5 oz) blueberries and 150 g (5 oz) raspberries.
Spoon over the top of the tartlets.

strawberry rosé jelly & syllabub

Serves **6**
Preparation time **25 minutes**,
  plus soaking and chilling

4 tablespoons **water**
1 sachet or 3 teaspoons
  powdered gelatine
40 g (1½ oz) **caster sugar**
500 ml (17 fl oz) **rosé wine**
250 g (8 oz) small
  strawberries, hulled and
  halved

Syllabub cream
finely grated rind of **1 lemon**
25 g (1 oz) **caster sugar**
6 tablespoons **rosé wine**
250 ml (8 fl oz) **double cream**

Spoon the measured water into a small heatproof bowl
or mug, then sprinkle the gelatine over the top, tilting
the bowl so that the dry powder is completely absorbed
by the water. Leave to soak for 5 minutes.

Heat the bowl or mug in a small pan of simmering
water for 5 minutes or until a clear liquid forms. Take
off the heat, then stir in the sugar until dissolved. Cool
slightly, then gradually mix into the rosé wine.

Divide the strawberries between 6 tall Champagne-
style glasses. Pour the rosé jelly mixture over and chill
in the refrigerator until the jelly is set.

Mix the lemon rind, sugar and wine for the syllabub
together and set aside. When ready to serve, whip the
cream until it forms soft swirls, then gradually whisk in
the lemon rind mixture. Spoon over the jellies.

For buck's fizz jellies, dissolve the gelatine as above,
add 25 g (1 oz) caster sugar and when cool mix
in 200 ml (7 fl oz) blood (or ordinary) orange juice
and 500 ml (17 fl oz) cheap dry sparkling white
wine. Divide 150 g (5 oz) fresh or frozen raspberries
between the glasses, then top up with the jelly. Chill
until set and serve plain.

summer berry sponge

Serves **6–8**
Preparation time **30 minutes**,
  plus cooling
Cooking time **10–12 minutes**

4 eggs
100 g (3½ oz) **caster sugar**
100 g (3½ oz) **plain flour**
finely grated rind and
  2 tablespoons juice of
  1 lemon
150 ml (¼ pint) **double cream**
150 g (5 oz) **fromage frais**
3 tablespoons **lemon curd**
500 g (1 lb) small
  strawberries, halved
150 g (5 oz) **blueberries**
4 tablespoons **redcurrant jelly**
1 tablespoon **water** (or **lemon
  juice**)

Whisk the eggs and caster sugar in a large bowl until
very thick and the mixture leaves a trail when lifted. Sift
the flour over the surface of the eggs, then fold in very
gently. Add the lemon rind and juice and fold in until
just mixed. Pour the mixture into a greased, floured
25 cm (10 inch) sponge flan tin, tilting the tin to ease
into an even layer.

Bake in a preheated oven, 180°C (350°F), Gas Mark
4, for 10–12 minutes until the top of the sponge
is golden and the centre springs back when lightly
pressed. Cool the sponge in the tin for 5–10 minutes,
then carefully turn it out on to a wire rack to cool.

Whip the cream until it forms soft swirls, then fold in
the fromage frais and lemon curd. Transfer the sponge
to a serving plate, spoon the cream into the centre,
spread into an even layer, then top with the strawberries
and blueberries. Warm the redcurrant jelly in a small
saucepan with the measured water (or lemon juice),
then brush over the fruit.

For strawberry sponge flan with Pimm's, make the
sponge flan as above, then fill with 300 ml (½ pint)
whipped cream flavoured with the grated rind of
½ orange. Top with 500 g (1 lb) sliced strawberries
and 150 g (5 oz) raspberries that have been soaked
in 3 tablespoons undiluted Pimm's and 2 tablespoons
caster sugar for 30 minutes.

summer berry mousses

Serves **6**
Preparation time **45 minutes**,
  plus cooling and chilling
Cooking time **12–15 minutes**

3 eggs
75 g (3 oz) **caster sugar**
75 g (3 oz) **plain flour**, sifted

Mousse
2 teaspoons **powdered
  gelatine**
2 tablespoons **cold water**
2 **egg whites**
75 g (3 oz) **caster sugar**
150 ml (¼ pint) **double cream**
200 g (7 oz) **frozen summer
  fruits**, just defrosted, puréed

To decorate
a few whole **redcurrants** and
  raspberries and some
  strawberries, halved
a few small **fresh mint leaves**
icing sugar, for dusting

Whisk the eggs and sugar until they are very thick and the whisk leaves a trail when lifted. Gently fold in the flour. Line the base and sides of a tin with a base of 35 x 25 cm (14 x 10 inches). Pour in the mixture.

Bake in a preheated oven, 180°C (350°F), Gas Mark 4, for 12–15 minutes until the sponge is golden and springs back when pressed. Leave to cool in the tin.

Cut 12 x 7.5 cm (3 inch) circles from the sponge with a biscuit cutter. Cut 6 strips of plastic (a new plastic folder is ideal) measuring 27 x 7.5 cm (11 x 3 inches). Wrap a strip tightly around each of the sponge circles and secure with tape. Put on a baking sheet.

Sprinkle gelatine over the measured water in a bowl and leave to soak for 5 minutes. Stand the bowl in a pan of simmering water and leave until the gelatine has dissolved to a clear liquid. Whisk the egg whites until stiff peaks form, then gradually whisk in the sugar until thick and glossy (see page 6). Whip the cream in a second bowl. Trickle the gelatine into the cream and mix together, then fold in the fruit purée and meringue.

Divide the mixture between the plastic collars, then top with the remaining sponge circles. Chill the mousses for 4–5 hours until set. Remove the plastic, scatter each mousse with a few whole or halved berries, dust with sifted icing sugar and serve.

For peach melba mousses, make the mousses with 4 ripe peaches, puréed and sieved. Chill as above, then serve drizzled with 125 g (4 oz) puréed, sieved raspberries and a few extra whole raspberries.

coffee latte custards

Serves **6**

Preparation time **20 minutes**, plus chilling

Cooking time **30 minutes**

2 **eggs**

2 **egg yolks**

397 g (13¾ oz) can **full-fat condensed milk**

200 ml (7 fl oz) **strong black coffee**

150 ml (¼ pint) **double cream**

cocoa powder, for dusting

chocolate wafer biscuits, to serve

Whisk the eggs, egg yolks and condensed milk in a bowl until just mixed. Gradually whisk in the coffee until blended.

Strain the mixture, then pour into 6 small 125 ml (4 fl oz) greased coffee cups. Transfer the cups to a roasting tin. Pour hot water into the tin to come halfway up the sides of the cups, then cook in a preheated oven, 160°C (325°F), Gas Mark 3, for 30 minutes until just set. Lift the cups out of the water, leave to cool, then transfer to the refrigerator and chill for 4–5 hours.

Whip the cream until it forms soft swirls when ready to serve. Spoon the cream over the top of the desserts, dust with a little sifted cocoa powder and serve with chocolate wafer biscuits.

For dark chocolate custards, bring 450 ml (¾ pint) milk and 150 ml (¼ pint) double cream just to the boil in a saucepan. Add 200 g (7 oz) plain dark chocolate, broken into pieces, and leave to melt. Mix 2 eggs and 2 egg yolks with 50 g (2 oz) caster sugar and ¼ teaspoon ground cinnamon, then gradually mix in the chocolate mixture and stir until smooth. Strain into small dishes and bake as above. Top with whipped cream and chocolate curls.

gooseberry fool with lemon thins

Serves **6**
Preparation time **30 minutes**,
  plus cooling
Cooking time **20–25 minutes**

500 g (1 lb) **gooseberries**,
  topped and tailed
75 g (3 oz) **caster sugar**
2 tablespoons **concentrated
  elderflower cordial**
2 tablespoons **water**
150 ml (¼ pint) **double cream**
135 g (4½ oz) can or carton
  custard

Lemon thins
50 g (2 oz) **unsalted butter**
50 g (2 oz) **caster sugar**
50 g (2 oz) **golden syrup**
grated rind 1 **lemon**, plus
  1 tablespoon of the juice
125 g (4 oz) **plain flour**
½ teaspoon **bicarbonate
  of soda**
icing sugar, for dusting

Cook the gooseberries with the sugar, cordial and measured water in a covered saucepan for 10 minutes until soft. Purée the gooseberries and their cooking juices in a liquidizer or food processor until smooth, or rub through a sieve. Leave to cool.

Whip the cream until it forms soft swirls, then fold in the custard and gooseberry purée. Spoon into small glasses and chill.

Heat the butter, sugar, syrup and lemon rind and juice for the biscuits in a small saucepan until the butter has melted and sugar dissolved. Stir in the flour and bicarbonate of soda and mix until smooth.

Drop teaspoons of the mixture on to 2 greased baking sheets, well spaced apart, then bake in a preheated oven, 180°C (350°F), Gas Mark 4, for 10–12 minutes until browning around the edges. Cool for 10 minutes, then loosen and transfer to a wire rack. Dust with sifted icing sugar and serve with the fool.

For nectarine & orange fool, chop the flesh of 4 ripe nectarines, then cook them in a covered saucepan with the sugar and 4 tablespoons of fresh orange juice (no water or cordial) for 10 minutes until tender. Purée and finish as above. Add the grated rind of ½ orange and 1 tablespoon juice to the biscuits instead of the lemon.

pavlovas with orange cream

Serves **6**
Preparation time **25 minutes**,
  plus cooling
Cooking time 1¼–1½ **hours**

100 g (3½ oz) **plain dark
  chocolate**, broken into
  pieces, plus a little extra,
  grated, to decorate
3 **egg whites**
175 g (6 oz) **caster sugar**
1 teaspoon **cornflour**
1 teaspoon **white wine
  vinegar**
½ teaspoon **vanilla essence**
250 ml (8 fl oz) **double cream**
2 **oranges**

Melt the chocolate (see page 6), then leave to cool for
10 minutes. Whisk the egg whites in a large bowl until
stiff, moist-looking peaks form. Gradually whisk in the
sugar and continue to whisk until the meringue is thick
and glossy (see page 6).

Mix the cornflour with the vinegar and vanilla essence,
then fold into the meringue. Add the melted chocolate
and fold together briefly for a marbled effect. Spoon
the meringue into 6 mounds on a large baking sheet
lined with nonstick baking paper, then swirl into circles
with the back of the spoon, making a slight indentation
in the centre.

Bake in a preheated oven, 110°C (225°F), Gas Mark
½, for 1¼–1½ hours or until the pavlovas may be easily
lifted off the paper. Leave to cool.

Whip the cream, when ready to serve, until it forms
soft swirls. Grate the rind of 1 orange and fold into the
cream. Slice off the top and bottom of each orange,
then cut away the rest of the peel. Remove the
segments, add any juice to the cream, then spoon this
over the pavlovas. Arrange the segments and grate a
little dark chocolate on top.

For strawberry & lychee pavlovas, make the
meringue as above, omitting the chocolate, and
bake for just 50–60 minutes. Fill with 250 ml (8 fl oz)
whipped double cream flavoured with the grated rind
of 1 lime and 2 tablespoons icing sugar. Top with
a 425 g (14 oz) can pitted lychees, drained and
quartered, and 250 g (8 oz) sliced strawberries.

vanilla crème brûlée

Serves **6**
Preparation time **20 minutes**,
   plus standing and chilling
Cooking time **25–30 minutes**

1 **vanilla pod**
600 ml (1 pint) **double cream**
8 **egg yolks**
65 g (2½ oz) **caster sugar**
3 tablespoons **icing sugar**

Slit the vanilla pod lengthways and place it in a saucepan. Pour the cream into the pan, then bring almost to the boil. Take off the heat and allow to stand for 15 minutes. Lift the pod out of the cream and, holding it against the side of the saucepan, scrape the black seeds into the cream. Discard the rest of the pod.

Use a fork to mix together the egg yolks and caster sugar in a bowl. Reheat the cream, then gradually mix it into the eggs and sugar. Strain the mixture back into the saucepan.

Place 6 ovenproof ramekins in a roasting tin, then divide the custard between them. Pour warm water around the dishes to come halfway up the sides, then bake in a preheated oven, 180°C (350°F), Gas Mark 4, for 20–25 minutes until the custard is just set with a slight softness at the centre.

Leave the dishes to cool in the water, then lift them out and chill in the refrigerator for 3–4 hours. About 25 minutes before serving, sprinkle with the icing sugar and caramelize using a blowtorch (or under a hot grill), then leave at room temperature.

For Amaretto brûlée, omit the vanilla pod. Mix the egg yolks and sugar as above, bring the cream almost to the boil, then immediately mix into the egg yolks adding 125 ml (4 fl oz) Amaretto di Saronno liqueur. Strain and continue as above. When chilled, sprinkle with 6 teaspoons flaked almonds, then the sugar, and caramelize as above.

blueberry & cherry cheesecake

Serves **6**

Preparation time **30 minutes**, plus chilling

Cooking time **5 minutes**

75 g (3 oz) **unsalted butter**
2 tablespoons **golden syrup**
175 g (6 oz) **digestive biscuits**, crushed
300 g (10 oz) tub **full-fat soft cheese**
200 g (7 oz) **fat-free fromage frais**
50 g (2 oz) **caster sugar**
grated rind and juice of
  1 **lemon**
½ teaspoon **vanilla essence**
150 ml (¼ pint) **double cream**

Topping
150 g (5 oz) **frozen blueberries**
150 g (5 oz) **frozen pitted cherries**
4 tablespoons **water**
2 tablespoons **caster sugar**
2 teaspoons **cornflour**

Melt the butter in a saucepan with the golden syrup, then stir in the biscuit crumbs and mix well. Tip the mixture into a greased 20 cm (8 inch) springform tin and press over the base and two-thirds of the way up the sides with the back of a spoon. Chill.

Scoop the soft cheese into a mixing bowl and break down with a spoon. Stir in the fromage frais, sugar, lemon rind and vanilla essence, then gradually mix in the lemon juice until smooth.

Whisk the cream in a second bowl until it forms soft swirls, then fold into the cheese mixture. Pour into the biscuit-lined tin and spread the surface level. Chill for 4–5 hours or overnight until firm.

Warm the frozen fruits in a pan with the measured water and sugar for 3–4 minutes until defrosted. Blend the cornflour with a little extra water, add to the pan, bring to the boil, stirring, and cook for 1 minute until the sauce has thickened. Leave to cool.

Loosen the edge of the biscuit case when ready to serve, unclip the tin sides, lift off the base and transfer the cheesecake to a serving plate. Cut into wedges and serve with the fruit compôte drizzled over the top.

For lime, kiwifruit & grape cheesecake, add the grated rind and juice of 2 limes to the cheesecake mixture instead of the lemon. Spoon into the tin as above, then arrange 2 sliced kiwifruits and 150 g (5 oz) halved green and red seedless grapes in rings over the top while the filling is still soft. Chill until set, then remove from the tin and cut into wedges to serve.

raspberry & champagne brûlée

Serves **6**
Preparation time **20 minutes**,
   plus cooling
Cooking time **25 minutes**

250 g (8 oz) **fresh
   raspberries**, plus a few
   extra, dusted with icing
   sugar, to decorate (optional)
6 **egg yolks**
150 g (5 oz) **caster sugar**
125 ml (4 fl oz) **dry
   Champagne**
125 ml (4 fl oz) **double cream**
3 tablespoons **icing sugar**

Divide the raspberries among 6 ramekin dishes. Put the egg yolks and sugar in a large bowl and set it over a saucepan of simmering water, making sure the water does not touch the bottom of the bowl. Whisk the egg yolks and sugar until light and foamy, then gradually whisk in the Champagne, then the cream. Continue whisking for about 20 minutes until the custard is very thick and bubbly.

Pour the custard over the raspberries and leave to cool at room temperature for about 1 hour. Sprinkle the tops with the sifted icing sugar and caramelize with a blowtorch (or under a hot grill). Serve within 20–30 minutes, decorated with a few extra raspberries lightly dusted with icing sugar.

For cidered peach brûlée, divide the diced flesh of 2 ripe peaches among 6 ramekins. Whisk the egg yolks and sugar as above, then gradually whisk in 125 ml (4 fl oz) medium cider instead of the Champagne. Continue as above.

gingered pineapple trifle

Serves **4–5**
Preparation time **20 minutes**

200 g (7 oz) **Jamaican gingercake**, diced
½ **fresh pineapple**, sliced, cored, peeled and diced
grated rind and segmented flesh of 1 **orange**
2 **kiwifruits**, peeled, halved and sliced
3 tablespoons **rum**
425 g (14 oz) can or carton **custard**
300 ml (½ pint) **double cream**
grated rind of 1 **lime**

Arrange the gingercake in an even layer in the base of a 1.2 litre (2 pint) glass serving dish. Spoon the pineapple, orange segments and kiwifruits on top and drizzle with the rum. Pour the custard over the fruit and spread into an even layer.

Whip the cream in a bowl until it forms soft swirls, then fold in half the orange rind and half the lime rind. Spoon the cream over the custard, then sprinkle with the remaining fruit rinds. Chill until ready to serve.

For raspberry & peach trifle, dice 4 trifle sponges and sprinkle in the base of a glass dish instead of the gingercake. Add 150 g (5 oz) fresh raspberries and the diced flesh of 2 ripe peaches. Drizzle with 3 tablespoons dry sherry, then cover with custard as above. Whip the cream and flavour with the grated rind of 1 lemon, spoon it over the custard and sprinkle with 2 tablespoons toasted flaked almonds.

florentine vanilla cheesecake

Serves **8–10**

Preparation time **25 minutes**, plus chilling

Cooking time **45 minutes**

125 g (4 oz) **plain dark chocolate**

50 g (2 oz) **slivered almonds**, lightly toasted

2½ tablespoons **glacé citrus rind**, finely chopped

6 **glacé cherries**, finely chopped

175 g (6 oz) **digestive biscuits**, crushed

65 g (2½ oz) **unsalted butter**, melted

480 g (17 oz) **cream cheese**

1 teaspoon **vanilla essence**

150 ml (¼ pint) **double cream**

150 g (5 oz) **Greek yogurt**

125 g (4 oz) **caster sugar**

3 **eggs**

Grease a 20 cm (8 inch) loose-bottomed cake tin and line the sides with a strip of nonstick baking paper. Chop half the chocolate into small pieces. Lightly crush the almonds and mix them in a bowl with the chocolate, glacé fruit, biscuit crumbs and butter. Stir the mixture until well combined, then turn into the tin, packing it into the bottom and slightly up the sides to form a shell.

Beat the cream cheese and vanilla essence in a bowl until smooth. Beat in the cream, yogurt, sugar and eggs to make a smooth batter.

Pour the egg mixture over the biscuit base and bake in a preheated oven, 160°C (325°F), Gas Mark 3, for 45 minutes or until the surface feels just firm around the edges but is still wobbly in the centre. Turn off the heat and let the cheesecake cool in the oven. Transfer to the fridge and chill well.

Transfer to a serving plate and peel away the lining paper. Melt the remaining chocolate (see page 6) and drizzle it around the top edges of the cheesecake. Chill until ready to serve.

For American cherry cheesecake, make a plain biscuit case by heating 75 g (3 oz) butter together with 2 tablespoons golden syrup in a pan until the butter has melted. Stir in 175 g (6 oz) crushed digestive biscuits and use to line the tin as above. Make the filling and bake as above. Serve topped with a 425 g (14 oz) can of cherry pie filling.

rosemary panna cottas

Serves **6**
Preparation time **15 minutes**,
   plus soaking and chilling
Cooking time **15 minutes**

3 tablespoons **cold water**
1 sachet or 3 teaspoons
   powdered gelatine
450 ml (¾ pint) **double cream**
150 ml (¼ pint) **milk**
4 tablespoons **thick honey**
2 teaspoons very finely
   chopped **rosemary leaves**

Apricot compôte

200 g (7 oz) ready-to-eat
   dried apricots, sliced
300 ml (½ pint) **water**
1 tablespoon **thick-set honey**
2 teaspoons very finely
   chopped **rosemary leaves**

To decorate
small **rosemary sprigs**
caster sugar, for dusting

Spoon the measured water into a small heatproof bowl or mug. Sprinkle the gelatine over and tilt the bowl or mug so that all the dry powder is absorbed by the water. Leave to soak for 5 minutes.

Pour the cream and milk into a saucepan, add the honey and bring to the boil. Add the soaked gelatine, take the pan off the heat and stir until completely dissolved. Add the rosemary and leave for 20 minutes for the flavours to infuse, stirring from time to time. Pour the cream mixture into 6 individual 150 ml (¼ pint) metal moulds, straining if preferred. Leave to cool completely, then chill for 4–5 hours until set.

Put all the compôte ingredients into a saucepan, cover and simmer for 10 minutes, then leave to cool.

Dip the moulds into hot water for 10 seconds, loosen the edges, then turn out the panna cottas on to small serving plates and spoon the compôte around them. Lightly dust the rosemary sprigs with caster sugar and use to decorate the panna cottas.

For vanilla panna cottas, make the panna cotta as above but without the rosemary, adding the seeds from 1 slit vanilla pod and the pod itself as the cream mixture cools. Discard the pod just before pouring the mixture into the moulds, then continue as above. Turn out and serve with fresh raspberries.

pink grapefruit cream

Serves **4**
Preparation time **15 minutes**

2 pink **grapefruits**
5 tablespoons **dark brown sugar**, plus extra for sprinkling
250 ml (8 fl oz) **double cream**
150 g (5 oz) **Greek yogurt**
3 tablespoons **concentrated elderflower cordial**
½ teaspoon **ground ginger**
½ teaspoon **ground cinnamon**
brandy snaps, to serve (optional)

Grate the rind of 1 grapefruit finely, making sure you don't take any of the bitter white pith. Cut the skin and the white membrane off both grapefruits, and cut between the membranes to remove the segments. Place in a large dish, sprinkle with 2 tablespoons of the sugar and set aside.

Whisk the cream in a large bowl until thick but not stiff. Fold in the yogurt, elderflower cordial, spices, grapefruit rind and remaining sugar until smooth.

Spoon the mixture into attractive glasses, arranging the grapefruit segments between layers of grapefruit cream. Sprinkle the top with a little extra sugar, add the brandy snaps, if desired, and serve immediately.

For spiced orange cream, finely grate the rind of 2 large oranges, then cut away the pith and membrane to release the orange segments. Sprinkle with 2 tablespoons of the sugar and set aside. Whip the cream, then flavour as above, adding the orange rind in place of the grapefruit rind.

peach & chocolate vacherin

Serves **6–8**
Preparation time **30 minutes**,
   plus cooling
Cooking time **1½–1¾ hours**

4 egg whites
125 g (4 oz) **caster sugar**
100 g (3½ oz) **light muscovado sugar**
150 g (5 oz) **plain dark chocolate**, broken into pieces

Filling
150 ml (¼ pint) **double cream**
150 g (5 oz) **Greek yogurt**
2 tablespoons **caster sugar**
3 ripe **peaches**, pitted and sliced

Line 2 baking sheets with nonstick baking paper and draw an 18 cm (7 inch) circle on each.

Whisk the egg whites in a large bowl until stiff, moist-looking peaks form. Mix the sugars together, then whisk in the sugar, a teaspoonful at a time, and continue whisking for 1–2 minutes until very thick and glossy (see page 6).

Divide the mixture between the lined baking sheets and spread into circles of even thickness between the marked lines. Bake in a preheated oven, 110°C (225°F), Gas Mark ¼, for 1½–1¾ hours or until the meringues may be easily lifted off the paper. Leave to cool in the switched-off oven.

Melt the chocolate (see page 6), then spread over the underside of each meringue, leaving about one-third of the chocolate in the bowl for decoration. Leave the meringues to harden, chocolate-side up.

Whip the cream, when ready to serve, until it forms soft swirls, then fold in the yogurt and sugar. Put one of the meringue circles on a serving plate, chocolate-side up, spread with the cream, then arrange peach slices on top. Cover with the second meringue, chocolate-side down. Decorate the top with the remainder of the melted chocolate, drizzled randomly.

For chocolate & chestnut vacherin, make the meringues as above. Spread with chocolate and leave to harden. Whip 150 ml (¼ pint) double cream, fold in a 210 g (7½ oz) can of sweetened chestnut purée and 150 g (5 oz) fromage frais, then fill the meringues.

lime & passion fruit crunch tart

Serves **6–8**
Preparation time **30 minutes**,
 plus chilling and freezing

100 g (3½ oz) **unsalted butter**
2 tablespoons **golden syrup**
250 g (8 oz) **digestive
 biscuits**, crushed
300 ml (½ pint) **double cream**
grated rind and juice of
 3 **limes**
400 g (13 oz) can **full-fat
 condensed milk**

To decorate
3 **passion fruits**, halved
150 g (5 oz) **blueberries**

Heat the butter and golden syrup in a saucepan, stir in the biscuit crumbs and mix well. Tip into a greased 23 cm (9 inch) springform tin, and press over the base of the tin with the end of a rolling pin. Chill while making the filling.

Whip the cream in a large bowl until it forms soft swirls. Add the lime rind and condensed milk and gently fold together, then gradually mix in the lime juice. Pour over the biscuit base and freeze for 4 hours or overnight.

Loosen the edge of the pudding from the tin with a round-bladed knife, remove the sides, then slide off the base on to a serving plate. Spoon the seeds from the passion fruits over the top, then scatter with the blueberries. Allow to soften for 30 minutes before cutting into slices to serve.

For chocolate orange crunch tart, make the biscuit base using chocolate digestive biscuits. Omit the lime rind and juice from the cream mixture, adding the grated rind and juice from 1 large orange instead. Freeze until solid, then decorate with 50 g (2 oz) plain dark chocolate, melted (see page 6) and drizzled randomly over the top. Return the dessert to the freezer until required.

pistachio & yogurt semifreddo

Serves **6**
Preparation time **40 minutes**,
  plus cooling and freezing
Cooking time **10–15 minutes**

4 **eggs**, separated
175 g (6 oz) **caster sugar**
grated rind of 1 **lemon**
1½ teaspoons **rose water**
  (optional)
200 g (7 oz) **Greek yogurt**
½ **fresh pineapple**, sliced,
  halved and cored

Pistachio brittle
150 g (5 oz) **granulated
  sugar**
6 tablespoons **water**
100 g (3½ oz) **pistachio nuts**,
  roughly chopped

Make the brittle. Heat the sugar and measured water in a frying pan until it dissolves, stirring gently from time to time. Add the nuts, then increase the heat and boil the syrup for 5 minutes, without stirring, until pale golden. Quickly tip the mixture on to a greased baking sheet and leave to cool. Break the brittle in half, then crush half in a plastic bag with a rolling pin.

Whisk the egg whites until very stiff, then gradually whisk in half the sugar until thick and glossy. Whisk the egg yolks in a second bowl with the remaining sugar until very thick and pale and the mixture leaves a trail. Fold in the lemon rind and rose water, if using, then the yogurt and crushed brittle, then the egg whites. Pour into a plastic box and freeze for 4–5 hours until semi-frozen and firm enough to scoop.

Cook the pineapple slices on a hot barbecue or preheated griddle pan for 6–8 minutes, turning once or twice until browned. Divide between the serving plates, top with spoonfuls of semifreddo and decorate with broken pieces of the remaining brittle.

For rocky road ice cream, make the brittle with almonds, hazelnuts and pecan nuts instead of pistachios. Whisk the egg whites, then the eggs and sugar, as for the semifreddo, then fold 135 g (4½ oz) ready-made custard and 150 ml (¼ pint) whipped double cream into the yolks with the crushed brittle. Fold in the egg whites as above, then freeze. Serve scooped into glasses with wafer biscuits.

cherry almond ice cream

Serves **6**
Preparation time **20 minutes**,
  plus cooling and freezing
Cooking time **20 minutes**

150 ml (¼ pint) **milk**
50 g (2 oz) **ground almonds**
1 **egg**
1 **egg yolk**
75 g (3 oz) **caster sugar**
2–3 drops **almond essence**
500 g (1 lb) **red cherries**,
  pitted, or **cherry compôte**
25 g (1 oz) **slivered almonds**
150 ml (¼ pint) **double cream**

Pour the milk into a small saucepan and stir in the ground almonds. Bring to the boil, then set aside.

Put the egg and the yolk into a heatproof bowl with the sugar and beat until pale and thick. Pour on the milk and almond mixture. Place the bowl over a pan of gently simmering water and stir until thick. Stir in the almond essence and leave to cool.

Purée the cherries in a food processor or blender (or use cherry compôte), then stir into the custard.

Toss the slivered almonds in a heavy pan over a low heat to toast them. Leave to cool.

Whip the cream until it forms soft peaks. Fold the whipped cream into the cherry mixture.

Transfer the mixture to a freezer container, cover and freeze until firm, beating twice at hourly intervals. Stir the slivered almonds into the mixture at the last beating. (If using an ice-cream machine, pour the cherry mixture into the machine, add the cream, churn and freeze. Once frozen, fold through the slivered almonds.) Serve the ice cream in individual glasses.

For strawberry & coconut ice cream, soak 50 g (2 oz) desiccated coconut in 150 ml (¼ pint) hot milk. Mix egg and egg yolk with sugar and make into custard as above, omitting the almond essence. When cold, fold in 500 g (1 lb) puréed strawberries and 150 ml (¼ pint) whipped double cream. Freeze as above. Serve with extra strawberries.

gingered apricot crush

Serves **6**
Preparation time **25 minutes**,
  plus cooling and freezing
Cooking time **10 minutes**

250 g (8 oz) ready-to-eat
  dried apricots
300 ml (½ pint) **water**
250 ml (8 fl oz) **double cream**
200 g (7 oz) **fat-free fromage
  frais**
40 g (1½ oz) **caster sugar**
75 g (3 oz) or about 4 pieces
  stem ginger from a jar,
  drained and roughly chopped,
  plus 2 tablespoons syrup
  from jar
40 g (1½ oz) **ready-made
  mini meringues**

Put the apricots and measured water in a saucepan, cover and simmer for 10 minutes. Purée the apricots and cooking liquid in a food processor or liquidizer until smooth, or rub through a sieve. Cool.

Whip the cream in a bowl until it forms soft swirls. Gently fold in the fromage frais, caster sugar, chopped ginger and ginger syrup. Crumble the meringues into pieces, then fold into the cream.

Line a 1 kg (2 lb) loaf tin with two pieces of clingfilm at right angles to each other so that the edges overhang the tin. Spoon in alternate spoonfuls of cream and apricot purée. Run the handle of a teaspoon through the mixture to marble together. Then fold the clingfilm over the top. Freeze for 6 hours or overnight until firm, or longer if preferred.

Unfold the top of the clingfilm and leave the dessert at room temperature for 15 minutes to soften slightly. Cover with a chopping board, invert the tin on to the board and remove the tin. Peel off the clingfilm. Cut into thick slices and serve.

For lemon & pineapple crush, flavour the cream mix with the grated rind of 2 lemons and a 220 g (7½ oz) can of pineapple, drained and finely chopped, instead of the ginger and ginger syrup. Add the meringues as above. Layer in the lined loaf tin with 4 tablespoons lemon curd and marble together. Freeze, then serve sliced with a drizzle of puréed strawberries.

chocolate ice cream

Serves **4**
Preparation time **20 minutes**,
  plus cooling and freezing
Cooking time **10 minutes**

300 ml (½ pint) **double cream**
2 tablespoons **milk**
50 g (2 oz) **icing sugar**, sifted
½ teaspoon **vanilla essence**
125 g (4 oz) good-quality
  plain dark chocolate,
  broken into pieces
2 tablespoons **single cream**

Chocolate sauce (optional)
150 ml (¼ pint) **water**
3 tablespoons **caster sugar**
150 g (5 oz) **plain dark**
  chocolate, broken into
  pieces

Put the double cream and milk in a bowl and whisk
until just stiff. Stir in the icing sugar and vanilla
essence. Pour the mixture into a shallow freezer
container and freeze for 30 minutes or until the ice
cream begins to set around the edges. (This ice cream
cannot be made in an ice-cream machine.)

Melt the chocolate (see page 6), together with the
single cream, over a pan of gently simmering water.
Stir until smooth, then set aside to cool.

Remove the ice cream from the freezer and spoon into
a bowl. Add the melted chocolate and quickly stir it
through the ice cream with a fork. Return the ice cream
to the freezer container, cover and freeze until set.
Transfer the ice cream to the refrigerator 30 minutes
before serving, to soften slightly.

Heat all the ingredients for the chocolate sauce, if
making, gently in a saucepan, stirring until melted.
Serve immediately with scoops of the ice cream.

For chocolate double mint ice cream, make the ice
cream as above, adding 2 tablespoons chopped fresh
mint and 20 g (¾ oz) crushed peppermint sweets to
the whipped cream and milk. Freeze as above, then
stir in the melted dark chocolate mix.

lychee & coconut sherbet

Serves **4–6**
Preparation time **30 minutes**,
   plus freezing
Cooking time **2–4 minutes**

425 g (14 oz) can **pitted
   lychees in light syrup**
50 g (2 oz) **caster sugar**
400 ml (14 fl oz) can **full-fat
   coconut milk**
grated rind and juice of **1 lime**,
   plus extra pared **lime rind**,
   to decorate (optional)
chocolate cups (see below),
   to serve (optional)
3 **kiwifruits**, peeled and cut
   into wedges, to decorate

Drain the syrup from the can of lychees into a saucepan, add the sugar and heat gently until the sugar has dissolved. Boil for 2 minutes, then take off the heat and leave to cool.

Purée the lychees in a food processor or liquidizer until smooth, or rub through a sieve. Mix with the coconut milk, lime rind and juice. Stir in the sugar syrup when it is cool.

Pour into a shallow plastic container and freeze for 4 hours or until mushy. Beat with a fork or blend in a food processor or liquidizer until smooth. Pour back into the plastic container and freeze for 4 hours or overnight until solid. (Alternatively, freeze in an electric ice-cream machine for 20 minutes, then transfer to a plastic box and freeze until required.)

Allow to soften for 15 minutes at room temperature before serving, then scoop into dishes or chocolate cups (see below) and decorate with kiwifruit wedges and pared lime rind curls, if liked.

For chocolate cups, to serve the sherbet in, melt 150 g (5 oz) plain dark chocolate over a pan of simmering water (see page 6), then divide between 4 squares of nonstick baking paper and spread into rough-shaped circles about 15 cm (6 inches) in diameter. Drape the paper over upturned glass tumblers, with the chocolate uppermost, so that the paper falls in soft folds. Chill until set, then lift the paper and chocolate off the tumblers, turn over and carefully ease the paper away.

fresh melon sorbet

Serves **4–6**
Preparation time **15 minutes**,
  plus freezing

1 **cantaloupe melon**,
  weighing **1** kg (2 lb)
50 g (2 oz) **icing sugar**
juice of **1 lime** or small **lemon**
1 **egg white**

Cut the melon in half and scoop out and discard the seeds. Scoop out the melon flesh with a spoon and discard the shells.

Place the flesh in a food processor or blender with the icing sugar and lime or lemon juice and process to a purée. (Alternatively, rub through a sieve.) Pour into a freezer container, cover and freeze for 2–3 hours. If using an ice-cream machine, purée then pour into the machine, churn and freeze until half-frozen.

Whisk the melon mixture to break up the ice crystals. Then whisk the egg white until stiff and whisk it into the half-frozen melon mixture. Return to the freezer until firm. Alternatively, add whisked egg white to the ice-cream machine and churn until very thick.

Transfer the sorbet to the fridge 20 minutes before serving to soften slightly or scoop straight from the ice-cream machine. Scoop the sorbet into glass dishes to serve. To make differently coloured sorbet, make up three batches of sorbet using a cantaloupe melon in one and honeydew and watermelon in the others.

For gingered melon sorbet, peel and finely grate a 2.5 cm (1 inch) piece of root ginger, then stir into the melon purée. Scoop into small glasses and drizzle each glass with 1 tablespoon ginger wine.

watermelon & tequila granita

Serves **6**
Preparation time **20 minutes**,
   plus infusing and freezing
Cooking time **2 minutes**

1 **vanilla pod**
150 g (5 oz) **caster sugar**
150 ml (¼ pint) **water**
2 kg (4 lb) **watermelon**
2 tablespoons **lemon juice**
4 tablespoons **tequila**

Use a small, sharp knife to score the vanilla pod lengthways through to the centre. Put it in a pan with the sugar and the measured water. Heat gently until the sugar has dissolved and let the syrup infuse for 20 minutes.

Slice the watermelon into wedges and cut away the skin. Blend the flesh in a food processor or blender until smooth, or rub through a sieve.

Remove the vanilla pod from the syrup, scrape out the seeds with the tip of a knife and return them to the syrup. Beat to disperse them. Discard the pod.

Strain the watermelon purée into a freezer container and stir in the vanilla syrup, lemon juice and tequila. Freeze for 3–4 hours until it is turning mushy. Mash with a fork and refreeze for 2–3 hours until it reaches the mushy stage again. Repeat the process once or twice more until the granita is evenly mushy. Freeze until required.

Fork through the granita to break up the ice and pile it into tall glasses. Serve with long spoons.

For blackberry and apple granita, heat 300 ml (½ pint) water with 25 g (1 oz) caster sugar until the sugar has dissolved. Add 4 large Gala apples that have been peeled, cored and diced and 150 g (5 oz) blackberries, then cover and simmer for 10 minutes. Cool, then purée and mix with 300 ml (½ pint) extra water. Freeze as above until flakes of ice begin to form.

mint granita

Serves **6**
Preparation time **20 minutes**,
  plus cooling and freezing
Cooking time **4 minutes**

200 g (7 oz) **caster sugar**
300 ml (½ pint) **water**, plus
  extra to top up
pared rind and juice of
  3 **lemons**
25 g (1 oz) **fresh mint**, plus
  a few sprigs to decorate
icing sugar, for dusting

Put the sugar and measured water into a saucepan, add the lemon rind and gently heat until the sugar has dissolved. Increase the heat and boil for 2 minutes.

Tear the tips off the mint stems and finely chop to give about 3 tablespoons, then reserve. Add the larger mint leaves and stems to the hot syrup and leave for 1 hour to cool and for the flavours to develop.

Strain the syrup into a jug, add the chopped mint and top up to 600 ml (1 pint) with extra cold water. Pour into a small roasting tin and freeze the mixture for 2–3 hours or until mushy.

Break up the ice crystals with a fork, then return to the freezer for 2–3 more hours, breaking up with a fork once or twice until the mixture is the consistency of crushed ice. Serve now, spooned into small glass tumblers, decorated with tiny sprigs of mint dusted with icing sugar, or leave in the freezer until required. If leaving in the freezer, allow to soften for 15 minutes before serving. If frozen overnight or longer, break up with a fork before serving.

For iced ruby grapefruit granita, make a plain sugar syrup as above, omitting the lemon rind. When cool, halve 4 ruby grapefruits, squeeze the juice and reserve 4 halved shells. Strain the juice into the syrup instead of the lemon juice, then freeze as above. Serve the dessert spooned into the reserved grapefruit shells.

lemon & honey ice

Serves **4–6**
Preparation time **20–25
minutes**, plus cooling and
freezing
Cooking time **2 minutes**

4 large or 6 medium **lemons**
about 4 tablespoons **water**
2 tablespoons **clear honey**
65 g (2½ oz) **caster sugar**
1 **fresh bay leaf** or **lemon
balm** sprig
450 g (14½ oz) **natural yogurt**
or **fromage frais**
strips of **lemon rind**, to
decorate

Slice off the top of each lemon. Carefully scoop out
all the pulp and juice with a teaspoon. Discard any
white pith, skin and pips, then purée the pulp and juice
in a food processor or blender, or rub through a sieve.
You will need 150 ml (¼ pint) – if there is less than
this, top it up with water.

Put the measured water, honey, sugar and bay leaf
or lemon balm into a saucepan. Stir over a low heat
until the sugar has dissolved, then leave to cool. Blend
the mixture with the lemon purée and the yogurt or
fromage frais. Don't remove the herb at this stage.

Pour into a freezer tray or shallow dish and freeze until
lightly frozen, then gently fork the mixture and remove
the herb. Return the ice to the freezer until firm.

Transfer to the refrigerator about 20 minutes before
serving. Serve decorated with strips of lemon rind.

For buttered oranges, to accompany the ice, peel
6 satsumas and, leaving them whole, place on a foil
square. Cut 50 g (2 oz) unsalted butter into 6 pieces,
add a piece to each orange with 1 teaspoon light
muscovado sugar and a pinch of ground cinnamon.
Wrap the foil to enclose the ingredients, then put on
a baking sheet and cook in a preheated oven, 180°C
(350°F), Gas Mark 4, for 10 minutes. Serve hot with
scoops of ice.

iced chocolate mousses

Serves **6**
Preparation time **30 minutes**,
  plus cooling and freezing
Cooking time **10 minutes**

250 g (8 oz) **plain dark
  chocolate**
15 g (½ oz) **unsalted butter**
2 tablespoons **liquid glucose**
3 tablespoons **fresh orange
  juice**
3 **eggs**, separated
200 ml (7 fl oz) **double cream**

Make chocolate curls by paring the underside of the block of chocolate with a swivel-bladed vegetable peeler. If the curls are very small, microwave the chocolate in 10-second bursts on full power (or place in a warm oven) until the chocolate is soft enough to shape. When you have enough curls to decorate 6 mousses, break the remainder into pieces – you should have 200 g (7 oz) – and melt (see page 6).

Stir the butter and glucose into the chocolate, then mix in the orange juice. Stir the egg yolks one by one into the mixture until smooth. Take off the heat and leave to cool.

Whisk the egg whites until softly peaking. Whip the cream until it forms soft swirls. Fold the cream, then the egg whites, into the chocolate mix. Pour the mixture into 6 coffee cups or ramekin dishes.

Freeze for 4 hours or overnight until firm. Decorate the tops with chocolate curls.

For chilled chocolate & coffee mousses, omit the chocolate curls and instead melt 200 g (7 oz) plain dark chocolate, then add 15 g (½ oz) butter (omit the liquid glucose), 3 tablespoons strong black coffee and 3 egg yolks. Fold in 3 whisked egg whites, then pour the mixture into 4 small dishes or glasses and chill in the refrigerator for 4 hours until set. Whip 125 ml (4 fl oz) double cream until it forms soft swirls, then fold in 2 tablespoons coffee cream liqueur, if liked. Spoon on to the top of the mousses and decorate with a little sifted cocoa powder.

chocolate apple pancakes

Serves **4**
Preparation time **10 minutes**
Cooking time **7–8 minutes**

40 g (1½ oz) **unsalted butter**
3 **dessert apples**, cored and
  thickly sliced
2 large pinches **ground
  cinnamon**
4 **ready-made pancakes**,
  about 20 cm (8 inches) in
  diameter
4 tablespoons **chocolate and
  hazelnut spread**
icing sugar, for dusting

Melt half the butter in a large frying pan, then add the
apples and fry for 3–4 minutes, stirring and turning
until hot and lightly browned. Sprinkle with cinnamon.

Separate the pancakes, then spread with chocolate
spread. Divide the apples among the pancakes,
spooning them on to cover half of each pancake. Fold
the uncovered sides over the apples.

Heat the remaining butter in the frying pan, add the
pancakes and fry for a couple of minutes on each side
to warm the pancakes through. Transfer to shallow
plates and dust with sifted icing sugar.

For peach melba pancakes, fry 2 large, thickly sliced
peaches in the butter instead of the apples, omitting
the cinnamon. Spread the pancakes with 4 tablespoons
raspberry jam, then add the peaches and fold. Warm
through, then serve sprinkled with fresh raspberries, a
dusting of icing sugar and a scoop of ice cream.

poached peaches & raspberries

Serves **6**
Preparation time **15 minutes**
Cooking time **25 minutes**

250 ml (8 fl oz) **water**
150 ml (¼ pint) **marsala** or
  sweet sherry
75 g (3 oz) **caster sugar**
1 **vanilla pod**
6 **peaches**, halved and pitted
150 g (5 oz) **fresh**
  raspberries

Pour the measured water and marsala or sherry into a saucepan, then add the sugar. Slit the vanilla pod lengthways and scrape out the black seeds from inside the pod. Add these to the water with the pod, then gently heat the mixture until the sugar has dissolved.

Place the peach halves in an overproof dish so that they sit together snugly. Pour over the hot syrup, then cover and cook in a preheated oven, 180°F (350°F), Gas Mark 4, for 20 minutes.

Scatter over the raspberries. Serve the fruit either warm or cold. Spoon into serving bowls and decorate with the vanilla pod cut into thin strips.

For poached prunes with vanilla, make the sugar syrup as above, then add 250 g (8 oz) dried pitted prunes instead of the peaches. Cover and simmer as above, then serve warm with spoonfuls of crème fraîche and 4 crumbled amaretti biscuits.

tamarind & mango sundae

Serves **4**

Preparation time **10 minutes**,
  plus cooling

Cooking time **8 minutes**

25 g (1 oz) **tamarind paste**

75 g (3 oz) **light muscovado
  sugar**

2 tablespoons **golden syrup**

grated rind and juice of **1 lime**,
  plus extra pared **lime rind**,
  to decorate (optional)

150 ml (¼ pint) **water**

2 teaspoons **cornflour**

15 g (½ oz) **unsalted butter**

1 large **mango**, pitted, peeled
  and cut into strips

12 scoops **vanilla ice cream**

Put the tamarind paste, sugar and golden syrup in a
small saucepan. Add the lime rind and juice and the
measured water and bring to the boil, stirring until the
sugar has dissolved. Simmer for 5 minutes.

Mix the cornflour with a little extra water in a cup, then
add to the sauce with the butter, bring back to the boil
and heat, stirring until thickened. Set aside to cool for
10 minutes.

Divide the mango and ice cream among 4 glass
dishes, then drizzle a little of the sauce over the top
and decorate with extra lime rind curls, if liked. Serve
the remaining sauce in a small jug.

For tamarind & banana yogurts, make the tamarind
sauce as above and leave until completely cold.
Roughly chop 3 bananas and mix with 400 g (13 oz)
Greek yogurt. Add the cooled tamarind sauce and mix
briefly for a marbled effect. Spoon into glass dishes
and serve.

pain perdu with mixed berries

Serves **4**
Preparation time **10 minutes**
Cooking time **10 minutes**

4 thick slices **brioche**
2 **eggs**
6 tablespoons **milk**
50 g (2 oz) **unsalted butter**
150 g (5 oz) **Greek yogurt**
250 g (8 oz) **raspberries**
100 g (3½ oz) **blueberries**
icing sugar, for dusting, or
    maple syrup

Cut each slice of brioche into two triangles. Beat the eggs and milk in a shallow bowl with a fork.

Heat half the butter in a frying pan. Quickly dip the bread, a triangle at a time, into the egg mixture, then put as many as you can get into the frying pan. Cook over a moderate heat until the underside is golden. Turn over and cook the second side, then lift out of the pan and keep hot.

Heat the remaining butter in the pan and dip and cook the remaining brioche triangles.

Arrange 2 triangles per serving on plates, top with spoonfuls of yogurt, a scattering of berries and a light dusting of sifted icing sugar or a drizzle of maple syrup. Serve immediately.

For spiced pain perdu with apricots, simmer 150 g (5 oz) ready-to-eat dried apricots with the juice of 1 orange and 125 ml (4 fl oz) water for 10 minutes until tender. Cut 4 slices of fruit bread in half. Mix the egg and milk as above with ¼ teaspoon ground cinnamon, then dip and fry the fruit bread as above. Arrange on plates with 150 g (5 oz) Greek yogurt and warm apricot compôte.

green fruit salad

Serves **6**
Preparation time **15 minutes**

300 g (10 oz) **seedless
green grapes,** halved
4 **kiwifruits,** peeled,
quartered and sliced
2 ripe **pears,** peeled, cored
and sliced
4 **passion fruits,** halved
4 tablespoons **concentrated
elderflower cordial**
4 tablespoons **water**
300 g (10 oz) **Greek yogurt**
2 tablespoons **runny honey**

Put the grapes, kiwifruits and pears in a bowl. Using a teaspoon, scoop the seeds from 3 of the passion fruits into the bowl. Mix 2 tablespoons of the cordial with the measured water and drizzle over the salad. Gently toss together and spoon into 6 glass tumblers.

Stir the remaining undiluted cordial into the yogurt, then mix in the honey. Spoon into the glasses. Decorate with the remaining passion fruit seeds and serve.

For ruby fruit salad, mix 300 g (10 oz) halved seedless red grapes with 150 g (5 oz) fresh raspberries and 150 g (5 oz) sliced strawberries. Sprinkle with the seeds from ½ pomegranate, then drizzle with 6 tablespoons red grape juice. Mix the yogurt with honey only, then spoon over the fruit salad. Decorate with a few extra pomegranate seeds.

sweet soufflé omelette

Serves **4**
Preparation time **15 minutes**
Cooking time **10 minutes**

375 g (12 oz) **strawberries**,
   hulled and thickly sliced, plus
   extra to decorate
2 tablespoons **redcurrant jelly**
2 teaspoons **balsamic
   vinegar**
5 **eggs**, separated
4 tablespoons **icing sugar**,
   sifted
25 g (1 oz) **unsalted butter**

Warm the strawberries, redcurrant jelly and vinegar together in a saucepan until the jelly has just melted.

Meanwhile, whisk the egg whites into stiff, moist-looking peaks. Mix the egg yolks with 1 tablespoon of the sugar, then fold into the egg whites.

Heat the butter in a large frying pan, add the egg mixture and cook over a medium heat for 3–4 minutes until the underside is golden. Quickly transfer the pan to a hot grill and cook for 2–3 minutes until the top is browned and the centre still slightly soft, making sure that the pan handle is away from the heat.

Spoon the warm strawberry mixture over the omelette, fold in half and dust with the remaining sugar. Cut into 4 and serve immediately with extra strawberries.

For sweet soufflé omelette with peaches & blueberries, put 2 ripe peaches, sliced, into a saucepan together with 100 g (3½ oz) blueberries, 2 tablespoons redcurrant jelly and 2 tablespoons lemon juice. Warm together, then make the sweet soufflé omelette as above, spoon over the warm fruit and serve immediately.

white choc & raspberry tiramisu

Serves **6**
Preparation time **20 minutes**

3 level teaspoons **instant coffee**
7 tablespoons **icing sugar**
250 ml (8 fl oz) **boiling water**
12 **sponge finger biscuits**, about 100 g (3½ oz)
250 g (8 oz) **mascarpone cheese**
150 ml (¼ pint) **double cream**
3 tablespoons **kirsch** (optional)
250 g (8 oz) **fresh raspberries**
75 g (3 oz) **white chocolate**, diced

Put the coffee and 4 tablespoons of the icing sugar into a shallow dish, then pour on the measured boiling water and mix until dissolved. Dip 6 biscuits, one at a time, into the coffee mixture, then crumble into the bases of 6 glass tumblers.

Put the mascarpone into a bowl with the remaining icing sugar, then gradually whisk in the cream until smooth. Stir in the kirsch, if using, then divide half the mixture between the glasses.

Crumble half the raspberries over the top of the mascarpone in the glasses, then sprinkle with half the chocolate. Dip the remaining biscuits in the coffee mix, crumble and add to the glasses. Then add the rest of the mascarpone and the remaining raspberries, this time left whole, finishing with a sprinkling of the chocolate. Serve immediately or chill until required.

For classic tiramisu, omit the raspberries and white chocolate from the layers. Mix the mascarpone with the cream and 3 tablespoons Kahlua coffee liqueur or brandy, then layer in one large glass dish with the coffee-dipped sponge finger biscuits and 75 g (3 oz) diced plain dark chocolate.

banana & muscovado ripples

Serves **4**

Preparation time **5 minutes**,
  plus standing

2 ripe **bananas**

juice of ½ **lemon**

15 g (½ oz) **crystallized** or
  glacé ginger, finely chopped,
  plus extra to decorate

150 g (5 oz) **low-fat natural
  yogurt**

8 teaspoons dark **muscovado
  sugar**

Toss the bananas in a little lemon juice and mash on a plate with a fork. Add the ginger and yogurt and mix together. Spoon one-third of the mixture into the bases of 4 small dessert glasses.

Sprinkle 1 teaspoon of the sugar over each dessert. Spoon half of the remaining banana mixture on top, then repeat with a second layer of sugar. Complete the layers with the remaining banana mixture and decorate with a little extra ginger, cut into slightly larger pieces.

Leave the puddings to stand for 10–15 minutes for the sugar to dissolve and form a syrupy layer between the layers of banana yogurt. Serve with dainty biscuits, if liked.

For banana, apricot & cardamom ripples, cook 100 g (3½ oz) ready-to-eat dried apricots with 150 ml (¼ pint) water and 2 roughly crushed cardamom pods, adding the pods and their black seeds, in a covered saucepan for 10 minutes until tender. Remove and discard the cardamom pods, then purée the mixture with 3 tablespoons fresh orange juice. Cool, then layer with banana and the yogurt mix as above. This can be served immediately.

summer fruit gratin

Serves **4**
Preparation time **10 minutes**
Cooking time **20 minutes**

2 ripe **peaches**, pitted
    and sliced
4 ripe **red plums**, pitted
    and sliced
150 g (5 oz) mixed
    raspberries and
    blackberries (or all
    raspberries)
200 g (7 oz) **mascarpone
    cheese**
4 tablespoons **caster sugar**
2 tablespoons **double cream**
grated rind of 1 **lime**

Arrange all the fruit in a shallow ovenproof dish. Mix the mascarpone with 2 tablespoons of the sugar, the cream and the lime rind, then spoon over the fruit and spread into an even layer.

Sprinkle the top with the remaining sugar, then put on a baking sheet and cook in a preheated oven, 190°C (375°F), Gas Mark 5, for 15 minutes until the cheese has softened and the sugar topping has caramelized. Serve immediately.

For tropical fruit gratin, arrange slices of 1 large mango in the dish with 1 sliced papaya and 150 g (5 oz) blueberries. Top with the mascarpone mix and bake as above.

baked apples & flapjack crumble

Serves **4**
Preparation time **15 minutes**
Cooking time **20–25 minutes**

4 **dessert apples,** halved and
  cored
75 g (3 oz) **raisins**
4 tablespoons **golden syrup**
6 tablespoons **apple juice**
  or **water**
50 g (2 oz) **plain flour**
50 g (2 oz) **rolled oats**
50 g (2 oz) **light muscovado**
  sugar
50 g (2 oz) **unsalted butter,**
  at room temperature, diced
2 tablespoons **sunflower**
  seeds
2 tablespoons **sesame seeds**

Arrange the apples, cut side up, in a shallow ovenproof
dish. Divide the raisins among the apples, pressing
them into the core cavity. Drizzle with 2 tablespoons
of the golden syrup and add the apple juice or water
to the base of the dish.

Put the flour, oats, sugar and butter into a small bowl
and rub in the butter with fingertips until the mixture
resembles fine breadcrumbs. Stir in the seeds. Spoon
the crumble over the top of the apples and mound up.
Drizzle with the remaining syrup.

Cook in a preheated oven, 180°C (350°F), Gas Mark
4, for 20–25 minutes until the crumble is golden and
the apples are soft. Serve warm with scoops of vanilla
ice cream or crème fraîche.

For plum & muesli crumble, halve 10 plums and
place them, cut side up, in an ovenproof dish. Drizzle
with 2 tablespoons honey and add 6 tablespoons red
grape juice or water to the base of the dish. Make the
crumble, using 75 g (3 oz) of muesli instead of the
oats and seeds. Bake and serve as above.

mini baked alaskas

Serves **4**
Preparation time **15 minutes**,
  plus freezing time
Cooking time **5 minutes**

4 slices **jam Swiss roll** or
  4 **trifle sponges**, separated,
  with the corners trimmed off
4 scoops **strawberry and
  vanilla ice cream** or **vanilla
  ice cream**
2 **egg whites**
50 g (2 oz) **caster sugar**
175 g (6 oz) **frozen summer
  fruits**, just defrosted or
  warmed in a small saucepan

Arrange the slices of Swiss roll or trifle sponge, well spaced apart, on a baking sheet, then top each with a scoop of ice cream. Put into the freezer for 10 minutes (or longer if you have time).

Whisk the egg whites in a large bowl until stiff, moist-looking peaks form. Gradually whisk in the sugar, a teaspoon at a time, and continue whisking for a few minutes until thick and glossy (see page 6).

Take the sponge and ice cream from the freezer and quickly swirl the meringue over the top and sides to cover completely. Cook in a preheated oven, 200°C (400°F), Gas Mark 6, for 5 minutes until the peaks are golden brown, the meringue is cooked through and the ice cream only just beginning to soften.

Transfer the baked Alaskas to shallow serving bowls and spoon the summer fruit around the base of the desserts. Serve immediately.

For cappuccino Alaskas, use chocolate Swiss roll (choose one without a chocolate outside coating) instead of the jam Swiss roll or trifle sponges. Top each slice with a scoop of coffee ice cream, then the meringue as above. When baked, dust lightly with sifted drinking chocolate powder and serve immediately.

caramelized clementines with bay

Serves **4**
Preparation time **10 minutes**
Cooking time **12 minutes**

250 g (8 oz) **granulated
  sugar**
250 ml (8 fl oz) **cold water**
8 **clementines**
4 small **fresh bay leaves**
6 tablespoons **boiling water**

Put the sugar and measured cold water in a saucepan
and heat gently, stirring very occasionally until the
sugar has completely dissolved.

Meanwhile, peel the clementines and, leaving them
whole, place in a heavy glass serving bowl or mixing
bowl with the bay leaves.

Increase the heat once the sugar has dissolved and
boil the syrup for 8–10 minutes, without stirring and
keeping a close watch on it until it begins to change
colour, first becoming pale golden around the edges,
then a rich golden colour all over.

Take the pan off the heat, then add the measured
boiling water, a tablespoon at a time, standing well
back in case the syrup spits. Tilt the pan to mix but
don't stir. Once the bubbles have subsided, pour the
hot syrup over the clementines and bay leaves. Leave
to cool, then serve the dessert with scoops of crème
fraîche or cream.

For caramelized clementines with whole spices,
omit the bay leaves and add 2 whole star anise or the
equivalent in pieces, 1 cinnamon stick, halved, and
3 cloves to the clementines. Make the syrup as above,
then pour it over the spices and fruit.

mulled wine pears

Serves **6**
Preparation time **10 minutes**
Cooking time **12 minutes**

300 ml (½ pint) cheap **red wine**
200 ml (7 fl oz) **water**
rind and juice of 1 **orange**
1 **cinnamon stick**, broken into large pieces
6 **cloves**
2 small **fresh bay leaves**
75 g (3 oz) **caster sugar**
6 **pears**
3 teaspoons **cornflour**

Pour the wine and measured water into a saucepan that will hold the pears snugly. Cut the orange rind into thin strips, then add to the pan with the orange juice, spices, bay leaves and sugar. Heat gently until the sugar has dissolved.

Peel the pears, leaving the stalks on, then add them to the red wine syrup. Simmer gently for 10 minutes, turning the pears several times so that they cook and colour evenly.

Lift the pears out of the pan and put on a plate. Mix the cornflour with a little water in a cup, then stir into the wine syrup and bring to the boil, stirring until thickened and smooth. Add the pears and leave to cool.

Transfer to shallow dishes with a rim and serve with spoonfuls of crème fraîche or cream.

For apples with cider punch, use sweet cider in place of the red wine, then add the orange rind and juice, spices and sugar as above, omitting the bay leaves. Dissolve the sugar, then add 6 dessert apples, peeled, cored and quartered. Simmer for 5 minutes until just tender, then thicken the syrup with cornflour as above.

moroccan baked figs with yogurt

Serves **4**
Preparation time **10 minutes**
Cooking time **10 minutes**

8 **fresh figs**, rinsed in cold
water
About 3 teaspoons **rose**
water
4 tablespoons **runny honey**
50 g (2 oz) **unsalted butter**
250 g (8 oz) **Greek yogurt**
a little **Turkish delight**, roughly
chopped

Cut a cross in the top of each fig and open out the cut
to halfway through the fruit. Arrange the figs in a small
roasting tin or shallow ovenproof dish. Add a few drops
of rose water to each fig, then drizzle with 3 tablespoons
of the honey and dot with the butter.

Bake in a preheated oven, 190°C (375°F), Gas Mark
5, for 8–10 minutes until the figs are hot but still firm.
Meanwhile, mix the yogurt with the remaining honey
and gradually mix in a little of the remaining rose water
to taste.

Transfer the figs to shallow serving dishes and serve
with spoonfuls of yogurt sprinkled with Turkish delight.

For orange & pistachio baked apricots, arrange
12 fresh apricots, halved, in a roasting tin. Add a few
drops of orange flower water to each apricot half, then
drizzle with 3 tablespoons honey and sprinkle with
40 g (1½ oz) halved pistachio nuts. Dot with 50 g
(2 oz) butter and bake as above. Serve with 250 g
(8 oz) Greek yogurt flavoured with 1 tablespoon
honey and orange flower water to taste.

white chocolate fondue with fruit

Serves **4**
Preparation time **10 minutes**
Cooking time **5 minutes**

200 g (7 oz) good-quality
  white chocolate, broken into
  pieces
300 ml (½ pint) **double cream**
2 tablespoons **kirsch**
2 **peaches**, cut into chunks
250 g (8 oz) large
  raspberries
375 g (12 oz) **strawberries**,
  halved
small bunch of **seedless red
  grapes**

Melt the chocolate together with the cream in a bowl set over a pan of gently simmering water (see page 6). Stir in the kirsch.

Arrange all the fruit on individual serving plates with forks or skewers for spearing the pieces.

Keep the fondue warm over a fondue burner while you dip and eat, or spoon the fondue into individual bowls, if preferred.

For dark chocolate & vanilla fondue, heat 200 g (7 oz) plain dark chocolate, 300 ml (½ pint) double cream, 4 tablespoons light muscovado sugar and 1 teaspoon vanilla essence together, stirring until smooth. Serve with 2 peaches, cut into chunks, 2 red-skinned dessert apples, cut into chunks, and 125 g (4 oz) marshmallows.

grilled strawberry zabaglione

Serves **4**
Preparation time **10 minutes**
Cooking time **10 minutes**

500 g (1 lb) **strawberries**,
   halved or quartered,
   depending on size
3 **egg yolks**
50 g (2 oz) **caster sugar**
6 tablespoons **dry** or **sweet**
   sherry
4 teaspoons **icing sugar**

Divide the strawberries among 4 shallow 300 ml (½ pint) ovenproof dishes, or use a large 1.2 litre (2 pint) dish if preferred.

Put the egg yolks, sugar and 4 tablespoons of the sherry in a large bowl and set over a pan of simmering water. Cook the mixture, whisking continuously using a hand-held electric whisk (or rotary hand or balloon whisk), for 5 minutes until the mixture is very thick and frothy and almost half-fills the bowl.

Add the remaining sherry and cook for a few more minutes until thick once more. Pour the mixture over the strawberries and sift the icing sugar over the top.

Cook under a preheated hot grill for 3–4 minutes until golden or caramelize the sugar with a cook's blowtorch. Serve immediately.

For fruit salad zabaglione, divide 125 g (4 oz) fresh raspberries, 125 g (4 oz) halved seedless red or green grapes and 2 peeled and diced kiwifruits among 4 glass tumblers. Make the zabaglione with 6 tablespoons dry white wine instead of sherry, and when just cooked pour over the fruit but don't grill.

citrus refresher

Serves **4**
Preparation time **10 minutes**
Cooking time **6–7 minutes**

150 ml (¼ pint) chilled **orange
    juice** from a carton
150 ml (¼ pint) **water**
125 g (4 oz) **caster sugar**
juice of ½ **lemon**
2 **ruby grapefruit**
4 **oranges** (a mix of **ordinary**
    and **blood oranges**, if
    available)
1 **orange-fleshed melon**
½ **pomegranate**

Pour the orange juice and measured water into a saucepan, add the sugar and heat gently until the sugar has dissolved, then simmer for 5 minutes until syrupy. Take off the heat and mix in the lemon juice.

Cut a slice off the top and bottom of each grapefruit, then cut away the rest of the peel in downward slices using a small serrated knife. Holding the fruit over a bowl, cut between the membranes to release the segments. Cut a slice off the top and bottom of the oranges, then cut away the rest of the peel. Cut into segments and add to the bowl.

Cut the melon in half, scoop out the seeds, then cut away the peel and dice the flesh. Add to the citrus fruit, then pour over the syrup. Flex the pomegranate to release the seeds, sprinkle over the salad, then chill until ready to serve.

For orange & fig refresher, make the syrup as above. Omit the grapefruit and increase the number of oranges to 6. Cut 4 fresh figs into wedges, peel and add to the oranges. Add the sugar syrup and sprinkle with some fresh mint leaves. Serve chilled.

index

acknowledgements

Executive Editor: Nicola Hill
Senior Editor: Fiona Robertson
Executive Art Editor: Leigh Jones
Designer: Jo Tapper
Photographer: Will Heap
Home Economist: Sara Lewis
Props Stylist: Liz Hippisley

Production Controller: Carolin Stransky
Commissioned Photography: © Octopus Publishing
Group Limited/Will Heap apart from the following:
© Octopus Publishing Group Limited: Gareth Sambidge
11, 13, 19, 33, 47, 95, 117; Ian Wallace 53, 57, 61, 63,
67, 69, 121; Jeremy Hopley 87, 91; Lis Parsons 99, 137;
Stephen Conroy 73, 107, 111, 115.